A WHO HQ GRAPHIC NOVEL

Who Smashed Hollywood Barriers with Gung Fu?

BRUCE LEE

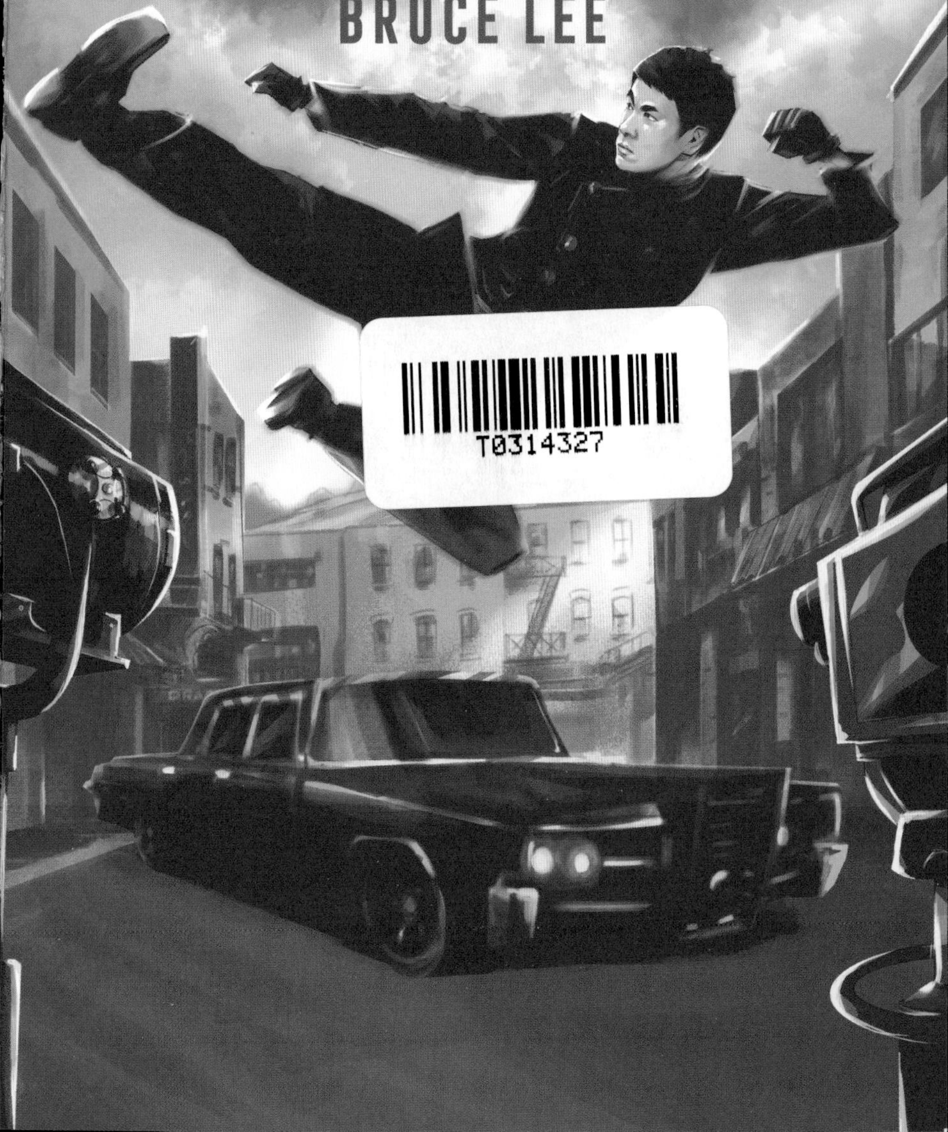

To Celina Sun for her guidance and to everyone breaking
racial barriers everywhere: thank you—TR

To the memory of Sifu Leon Trescott; the lessons he taught
I will always carry with me—RI

PENGUIN WORKSHOP
An imprint of Penguin Random House LLC
1745 Broadway, New York, New York 10019

First published in the United States of America by Penguin Workshop,
an imprint of Penguin Random House LLC, 2025

Visit us online at penguinrandomhouse.com.

Library of Congress Cataloging-in-Publication Data is available.

Manufactured in Italy

ISBN 9780593384626 (pbk)
ISBN 9780593384633 (hc)

10 9 8 7 6 5 4 3 2 1 LEG
10 9 8 7 6 5 4 3 2 1 LEG

Lettering by Comicraft
Design by Taylor Abatiell

This is a work of nonfiction. All of the events that unfold in the narrative
are rooted in historical fact. Some dialogue and characters have been fictionalized
in order to illustrate or teach a historical point.

For more information about your favorite historical figures, places, and events,
please visit whohq.com.

A WHO HQ GRAPHIC NOVEL

Who Smashed Hollywood Barriers with Gung Fu?

BRUCE LEE

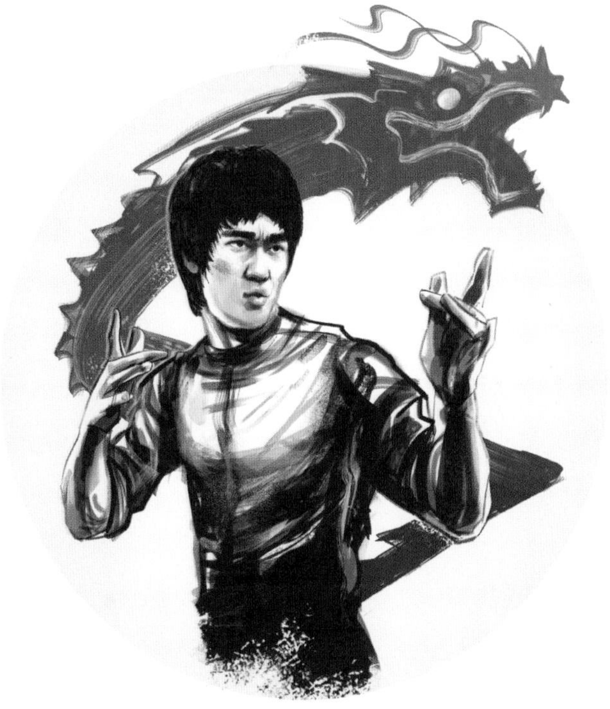

by Teresa Robeson
illustrated by Ryan Inzana

Penguin Workshop

Introduction

Although he's now considered a martial arts legend in the world of movies and television, Bruce Lee was not always a household name. Given the Chinese name "Jun Fan" when he was born on November 27, 1940, in San Francisco, California, Bruce grew up in his parents' hometown of Hong Kong.

As a kid, Bruce was so full of energy that his nickname was "Never Sits Still." His active personality and restless nature got him into many fights. To learn how to focus and protect himself, he took lessons in Chinese martial arts—known as gung fu in Cantonese or kung fu in English. The training was tough, but Bruce wanted to be an expert, so he pushed himself to become good at gung fu in a short period of time.

However, he continued to get into trouble, so when he turned

eighteen, his parents decided to send him back to the United States for a fresh start.

In Seattle, Washington, Bruce continued to practice gung fu, both while finishing high school and attending college, where he met and married Linda Emery. Around this time, he also started teaching others gung fu and opened his own studio in 1963.

Martial arts were becoming very popular in the United States, and people were interested in learning them. Bruce wanted to make gung fu as well-known as karate, and he imagined opening gung fu schools all over the country.

Which was why, as the year 1965 began, he was not expecting the phone call that would propel him to stardom.

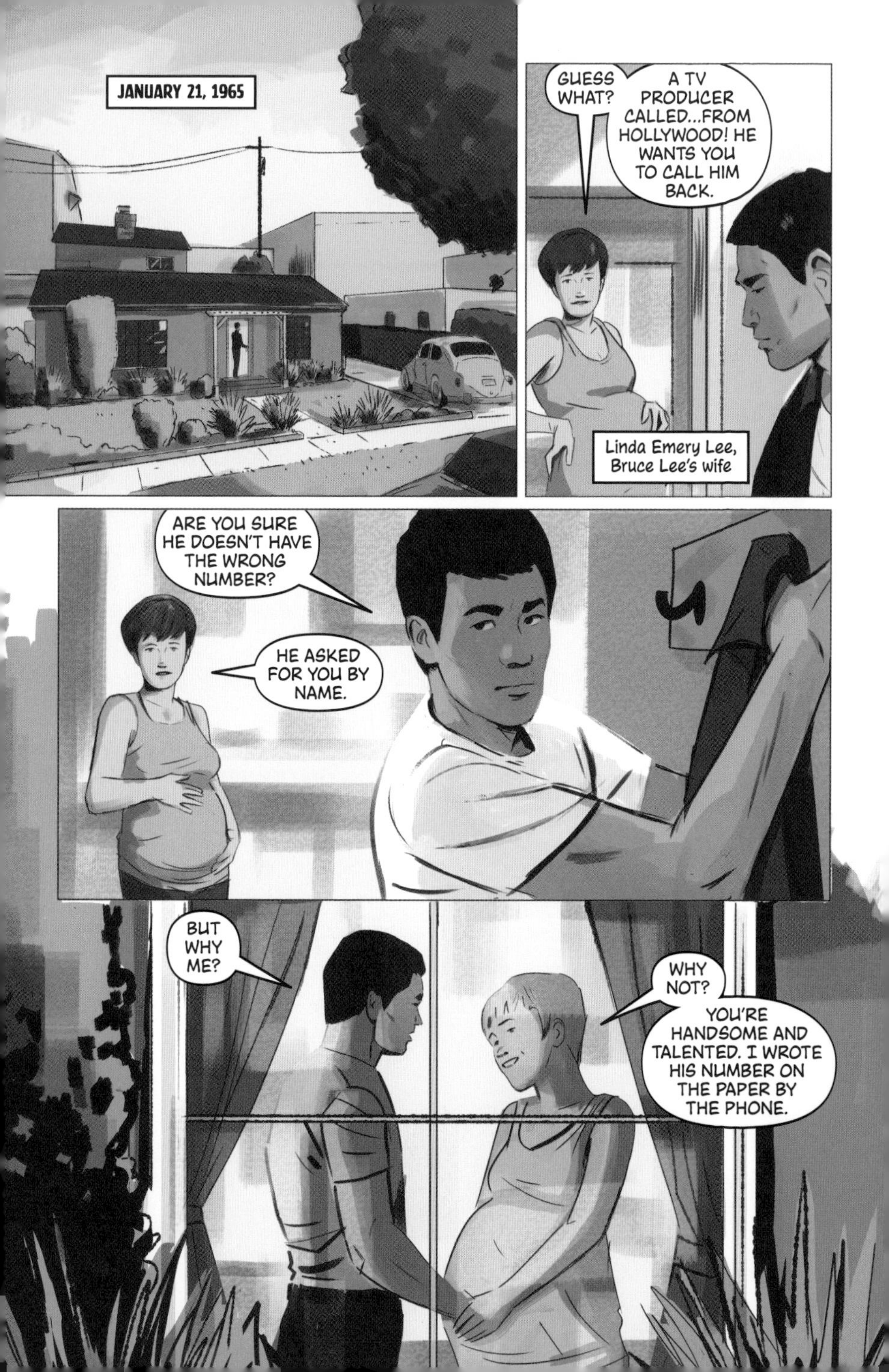

JANUARY 21, 1965
GUESS WHAT?
A TV PRODUCER CALLED...FROM HOLLYWOOD! HE WANTS YOU TO CALL HIM BACK.
Linda Emery Lee, Bruce Lee's wife
ARE YOU SURE HE DOESN'T HAVE THE WRONG NUMBER?
HE ASKED FOR YOU BY NAME.
BUT WHY ME?
WHY NOT?
YOU'RE HANDSOME AND TALENTED. I WROTE HIS NUMBER ON THE PAPER BY THE PHONE.

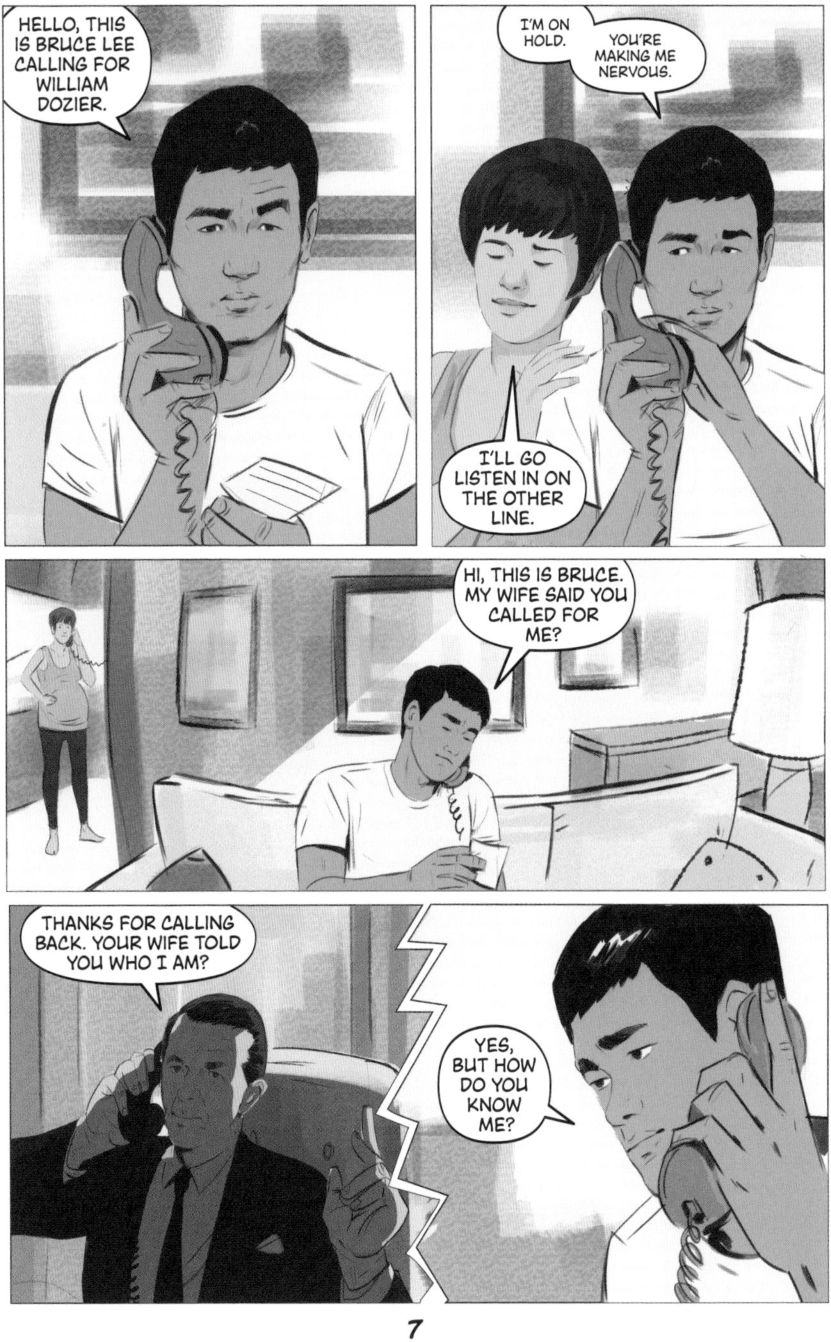
HELLO, THIS IS BRUCE LEE CALLING FOR WILLIAM DOZIER.
I'M ON HOLD.
YOU'RE MAKING ME NERVOUS.
I'LL GO LISTEN IN ON THE OTHER LINE.
HI, THIS IS BRUCE. MY WIFE SAID YOU CALLED FOR ME?
THANKS FOR CALLING BACK. YOUR WIFE TOLD YOU WHO I AM?
YES, BUT HOW DO YOU KNOW ME?

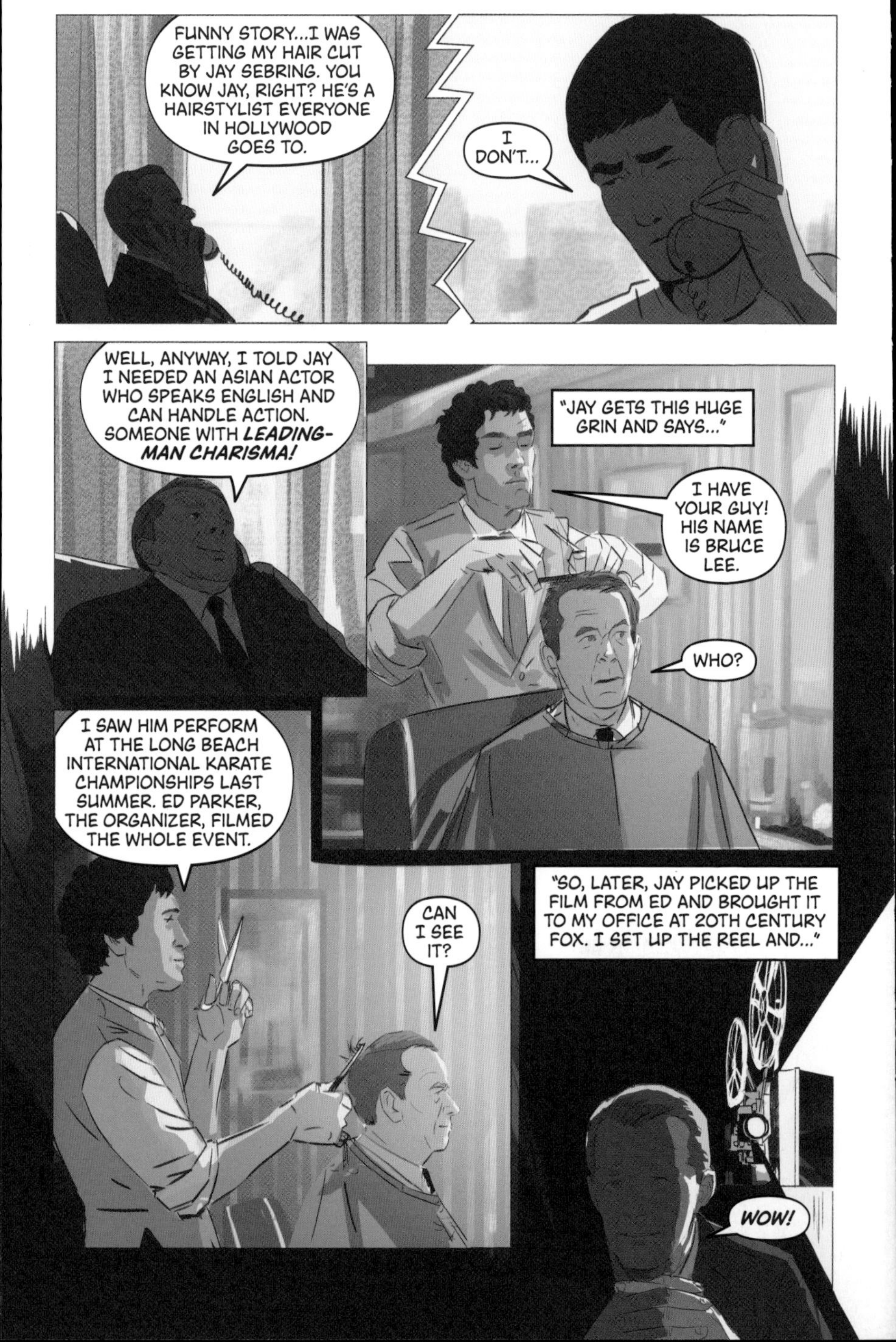
FUNNY STORY...I WAS GETTING MY HAIR CUT BY JAY SEBRING. YOU KNOW JAY, RIGHT? HE'S A HAIRSTYLIST EVERYONE IN HOLLYWOOD GOES TO.
I DON'T...
WELL, ANYWAY, I TOLD JAY I NEEDED AN ASIAN ACTOR WHO SPEAKS ENGLISH AND CAN HANDLE ACTION. SOMEONE WITH ***LEADING-MAN CHARISMA!***
"JAY GETS THIS HUGE GRIN AND SAYS..."
I HAVE YOUR GUY! HIS NAME IS BRUCE LEE.
WHO?
I SAW HIM PERFORM AT THE LONG BEACH INTERNATIONAL KARATE CHAMPIONSHIPS LAST SUMMER. ED PARKER, THE ORGANIZER, FILMED THE WHOLE EVENT.
CAN I SEE IT?
"SO, LATER, JAY PICKED UP THE FILM FROM ED AND BROUGHT IT TO MY OFFICE AT 20TH CENTURY FOX. I SET UP THE REEL AND..."
WOW!

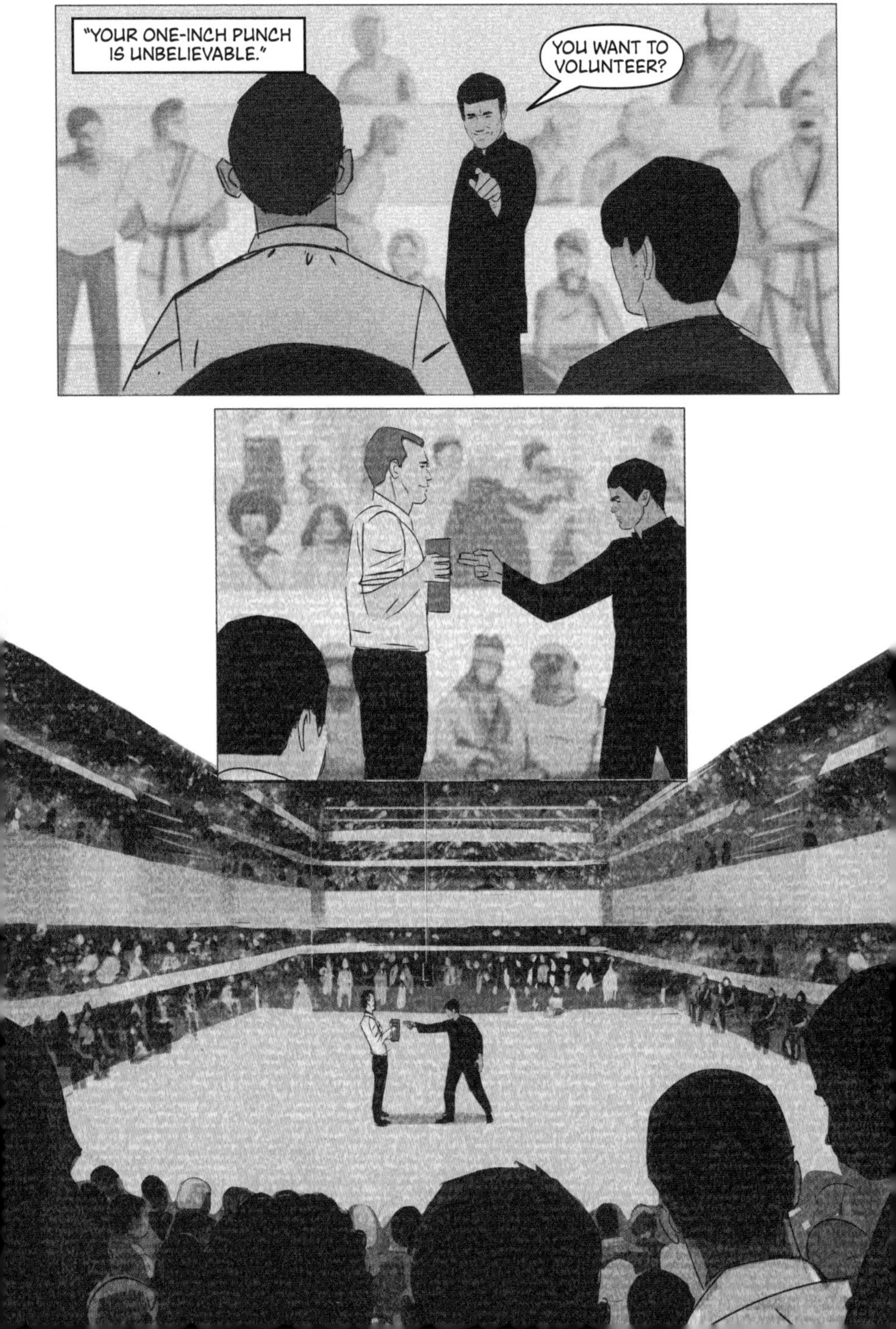
"YOUR ONE-INCH PUNCH IS UNBELIEVABLE."
YOU WANT TO VOLUNTEER?

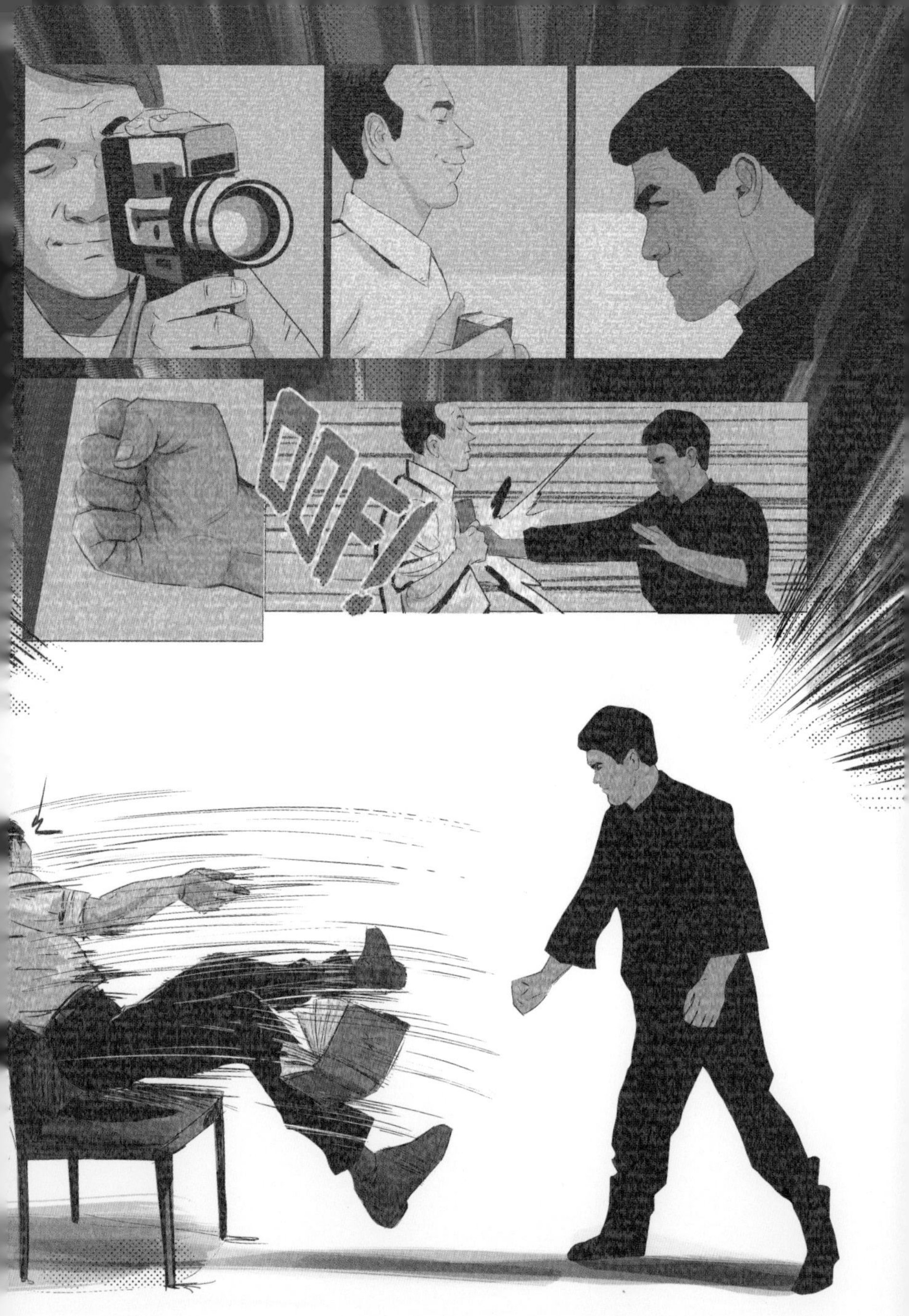
OOF!

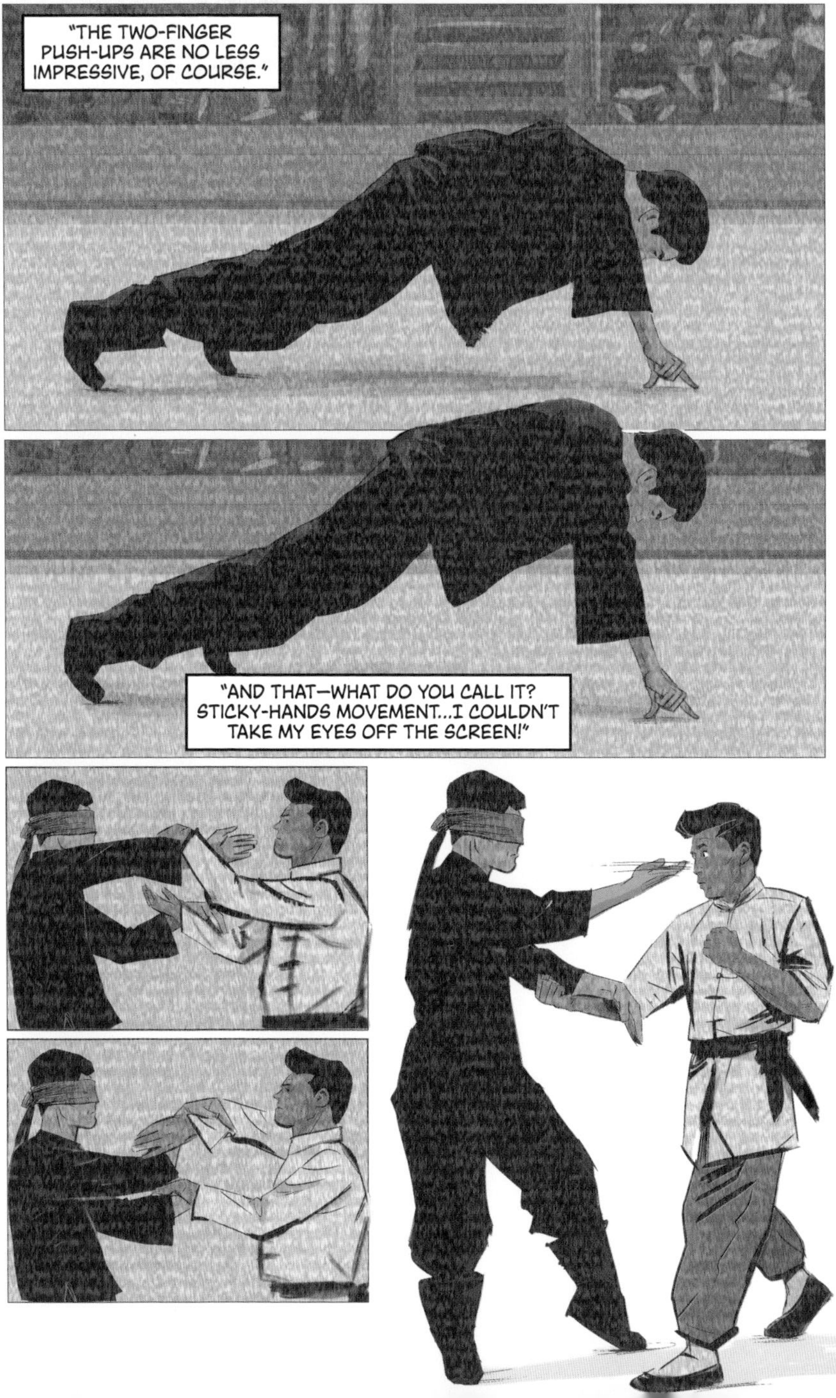
"THE TWO-FINGER PUSH-UPS ARE NO LESS IMPRESSIVE, OF COURSE."
"AND THAT—WHAT DO YOU CALL IT? STICKY-HANDS MOVEMENT...I COULDN'T TAKE MY EYES OFF THE SCREEN!"

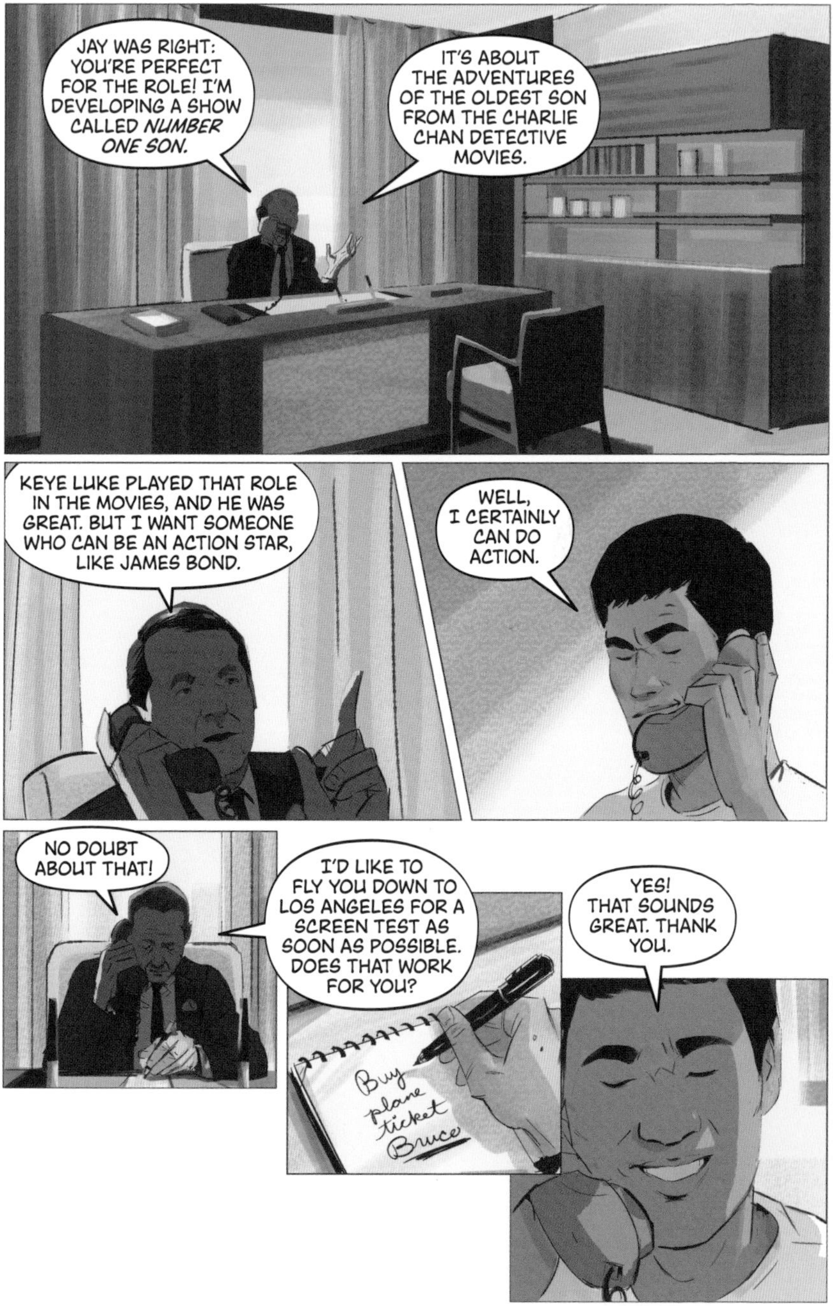
JAY WAS RIGHT: YOU'RE PERFECT FOR THE ROLE! I'M DEVELOPING A SHOW CALLED *NUMBER ONE SON.*
IT'S ABOUT THE ADVENTURES OF THE OLDEST SON FROM THE CHARLIE CHAN DETECTIVE MOVIES.
KEYE LUKE PLAYED THAT ROLE IN THE MOVIES, AND HE WAS GREAT. BUT I WANT SOMEONE WHO CAN BE AN ACTION STAR, LIKE JAMES BOND.
WELL, I CERTAINLY CAN DO ACTION.
NO DOUBT ABOUT THAT!
I'D LIKE TO FLY YOU DOWN TO LOS ANGELES FOR A SCREEN TEST AS SOON AS POSSIBLE. DOES THAT WORK FOR YOU?
Buy plane ticket Bruce
YES! THAT SOUNDS GREAT. THANK YOU.

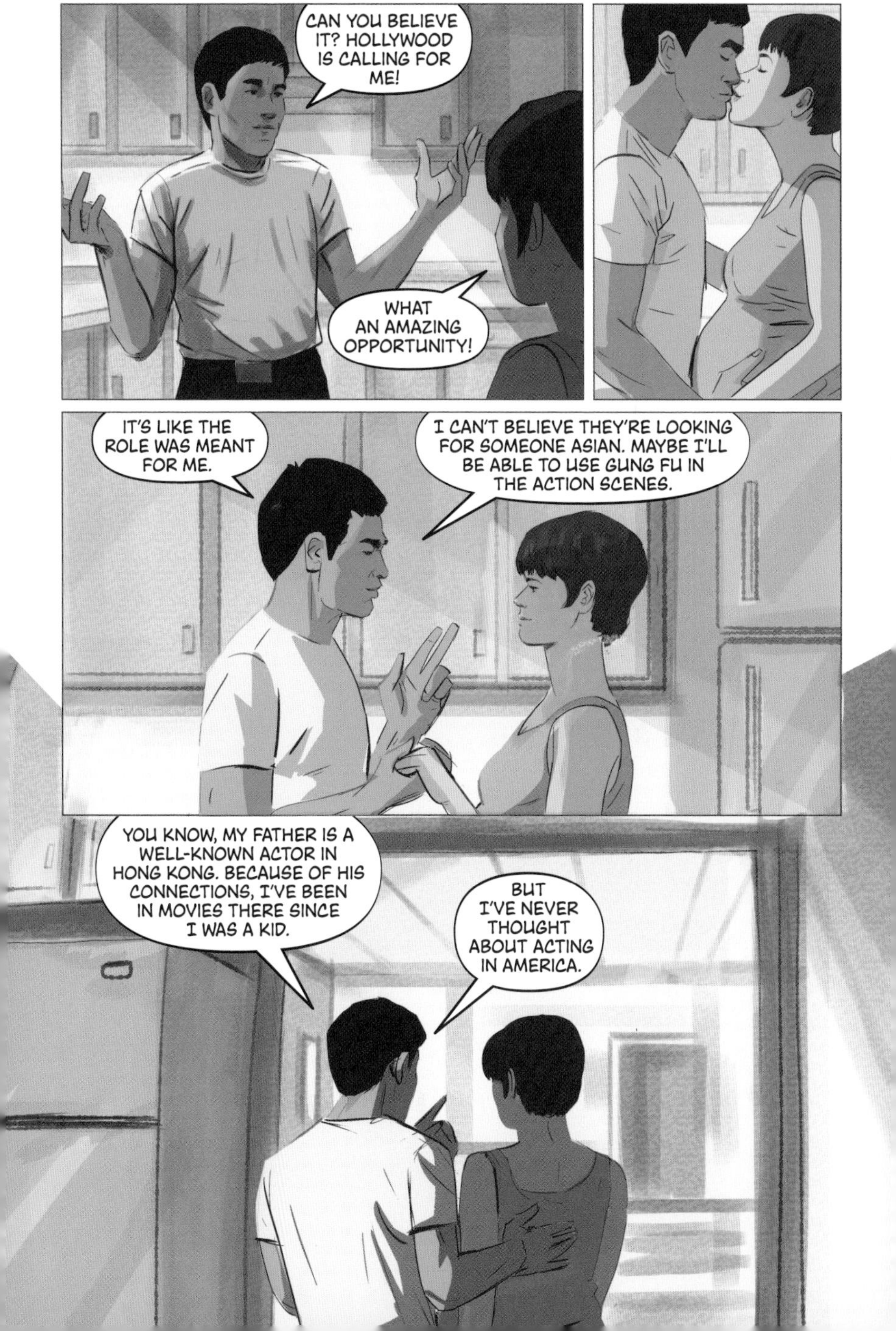
CAN YOU BELIEVE IT? HOLLYWOOD IS CALLING FOR ME!
WHAT AN AMAZING OPPORTUNITY!
IT'S LIKE THE ROLE WAS MEANT FOR ME.
I CAN'T BELIEVE THEY'RE LOOKING FOR SOMEONE ASIAN. MAYBE I'LL BE ABLE TO USE GUNG FU IN THE ACTION SCENES.
YOU KNOW, MY FATHER IS A WELL-KNOWN ACTOR IN HONG KONG. BECAUSE OF HIS CONNECTIONS, I'VE BEEN IN MOVIES THERE SINCE I WAS A KID.
BUT I'VE NEVER THOUGHT ABOUT ACTING IN AMERICA.

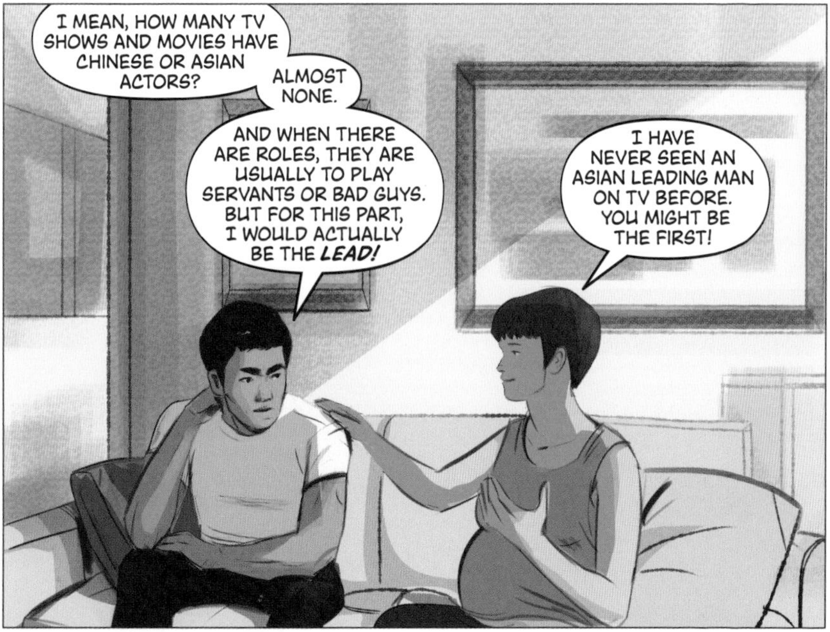
I MEAN, HOW MANY TV SHOWS AND MOVIES HAVE CHINESE OR ASIAN ACTORS?
ALMOST NONE.
AND WHEN THERE ARE ROLES, THEY ARE USUALLY TO PLAY SERVANTS OR BAD GUYS. BUT FOR THIS PART, I WOULD ACTUALLY BE THE LEAD!
I HAVE NEVER SEEN AN ASIAN LEADING MAN ON TV BEFORE. YOU MIGHT BE THE FIRST!

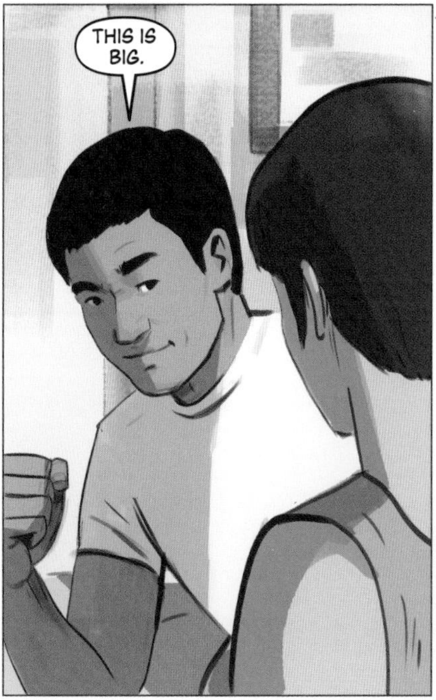
THIS IS BIG.

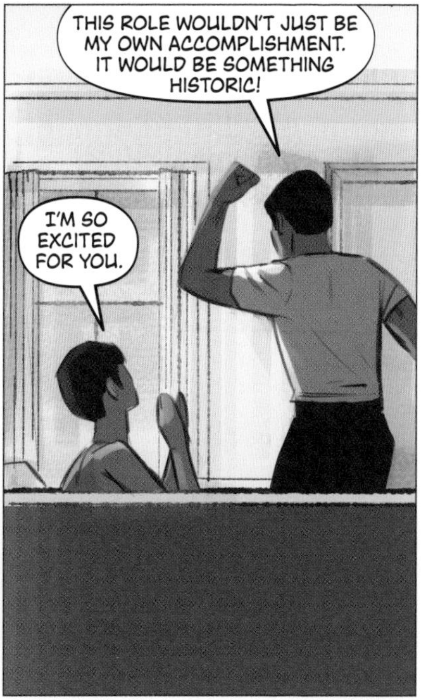
THIS ROLE WOULDN'T JUST BE MY OWN ACCOMPLISHMENT. IT WOULD BE SOMETHING HISTORIC!
I'M SO EXCITED FOR YOU.

Linda Emery Lee

Born on March 21, 1945, in Everett, Washington, Linda Emery grew up in nearby Seattle. Because her family was poor, Linda wanted to attend university and become a doctor so she could earn better money while also helping others.

Linda met Bruce while they were both at college. Bruce taught a gung fu class that Linda's friend introduced her to. Soon, she and Bruce started dating, though Linda hid this from her family who, she knew, wouldn't approve of her relationship with an Asian man.

The two married on August 17, 1964—three years before interracial marriage was officially legal across the United States. Both their families weren't happy about the marriage at first, but they came to accept it. After marrying Bruce, Linda became a housewife, taking care of their children and managing their home.

Bruce once said to friends that he and Linda were "two halves that make a whole." Linda felt the same, describing Bruce as a man of "quality, and integrity, and great love, and warmth."

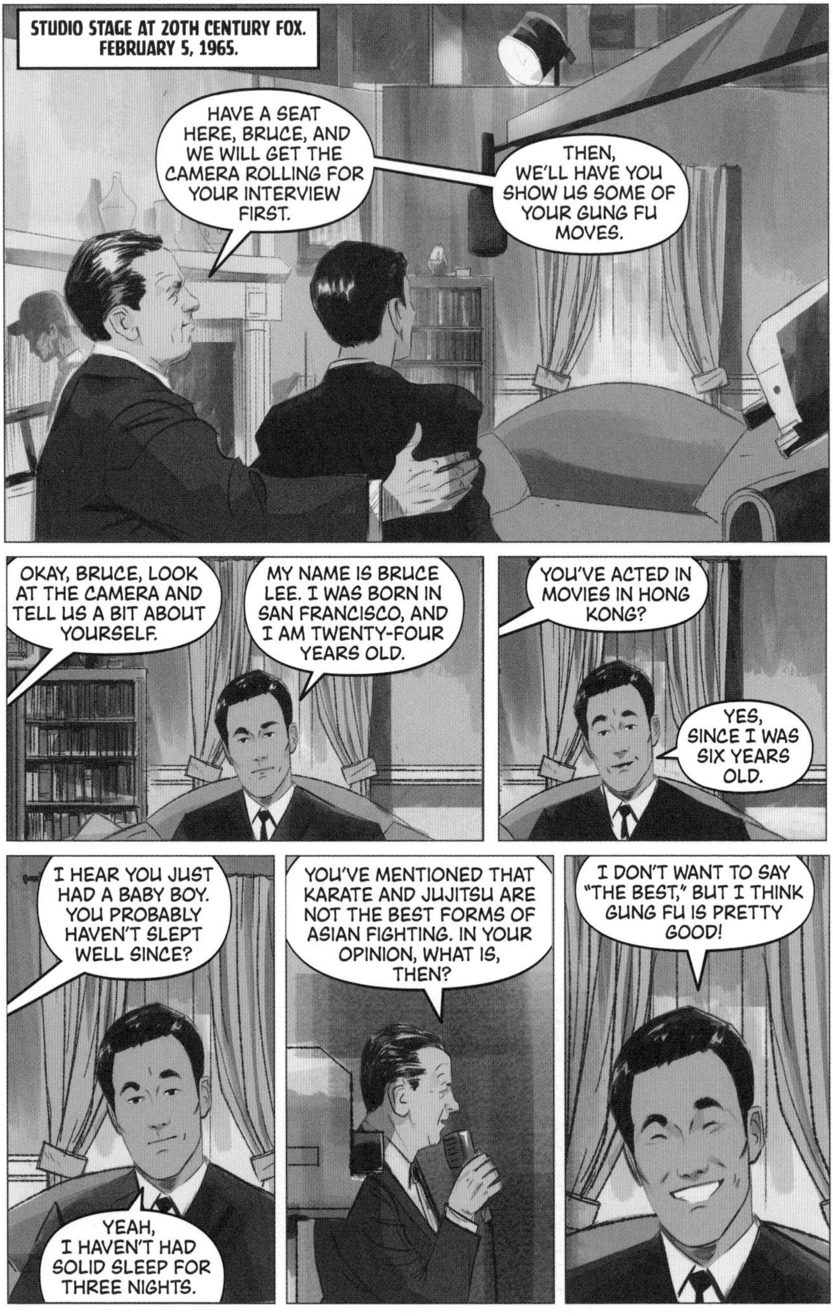
STUDIO STAGE AT 20TH CENTURY FOX. FEBRUARY 5, 1965.
HAVE A SEAT HERE, BRUCE, AND WE WILL GET THE CAMERA ROLLING FOR YOUR INTERVIEW FIRST.
THEN, WE'LL HAVE YOU SHOW US SOME OF YOUR GUNG FU MOVES.
OKAY, BRUCE, LOOK AT THE CAMERA AND TELL US A BIT ABOUT YOURSELF.
MY NAME IS BRUCE LEE. I WAS BORN IN SAN FRANCISCO, AND I AM TWENTY-FOUR YEARS OLD.
YOU'VE ACTED IN MOVIES IN HONG KONG?
YES, SINCE I WAS SIX YEARS OLD.
I HEAR YOU JUST HAD A BABY BOY. YOU PROBABLY HAVEN'T SLEPT WELL SINCE?
YEAH, I HAVEN'T HAD SOLID SLEEP FOR THREE NIGHTS.
YOU'VE MENTIONED THAT KARATE AND JUJITSU ARE NOT THE BEST FORMS OF ASIAN FIGHTING. IN YOUR OPINION, WHAT IS, THEN?
I DON'T WANT TO SAY "THE BEST," BUT I THINK GUNG FU IS PRETTY GOOD!

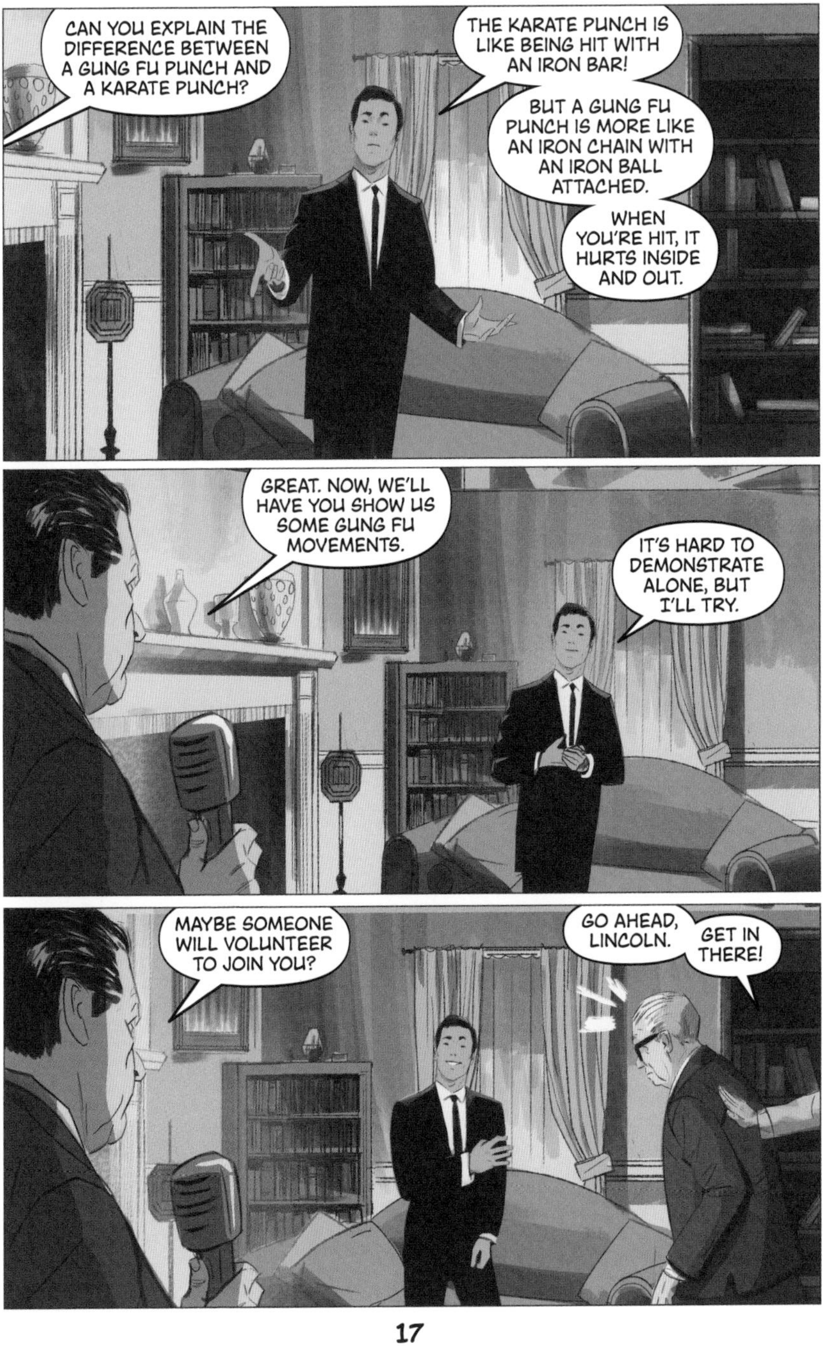
CAN YOU EXPLAIN THE DIFFERENCE BETWEEN A GUNG FU PUNCH AND A KARATE PUNCH?
THE KARATE PUNCH IS LIKE BEING HIT WITH AN IRON BAR!
BUT A GUNG FU PUNCH IS MORE LIKE AN IRON CHAIN WITH AN IRON BALL ATTACHED.
WHEN YOU'RE HIT, IT HURTS INSIDE AND OUT.
GREAT. NOW, WE'LL HAVE YOU SHOW US SOME GUNG FU MOVEMENTS.
IT'S HARD TO DEMONSTRATE ALONE, BUT I'LL TRY.
MAYBE SOMEONE WILL VOLUNTEER TO JOIN YOU?
GO AHEAD, LINCOLN.
GET IN THERE!

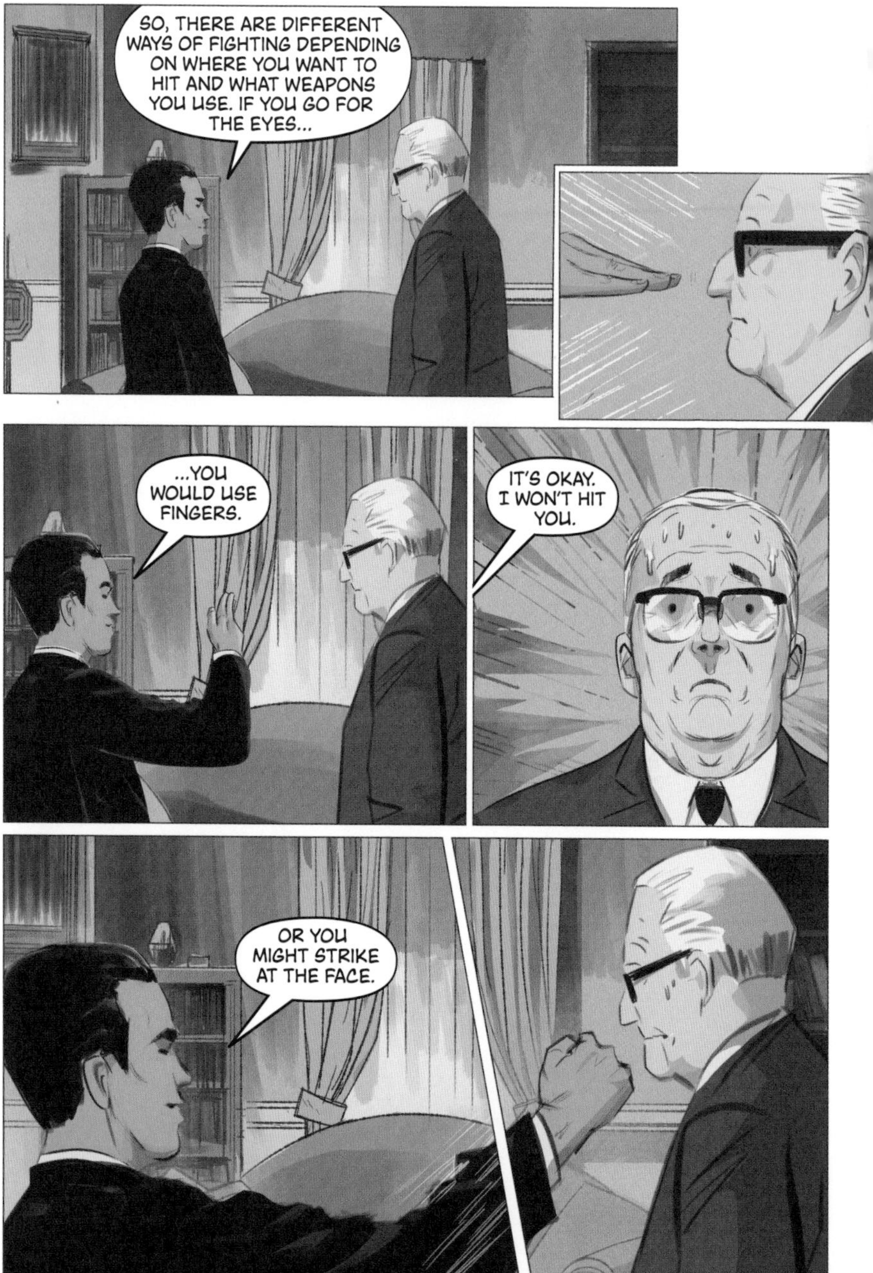
SO, THERE ARE DIFFERENT WAYS OF FIGHTING DEPENDING ON WHERE YOU WANT TO HIT AND WHAT WEAPONS YOU USE. IF YOU GO FOR THE EYES...
...YOU WOULD USE FINGERS.
IT'S OKAY. I WON'T HIT YOU.
OR YOU MIGHT STRIKE AT THE FACE.

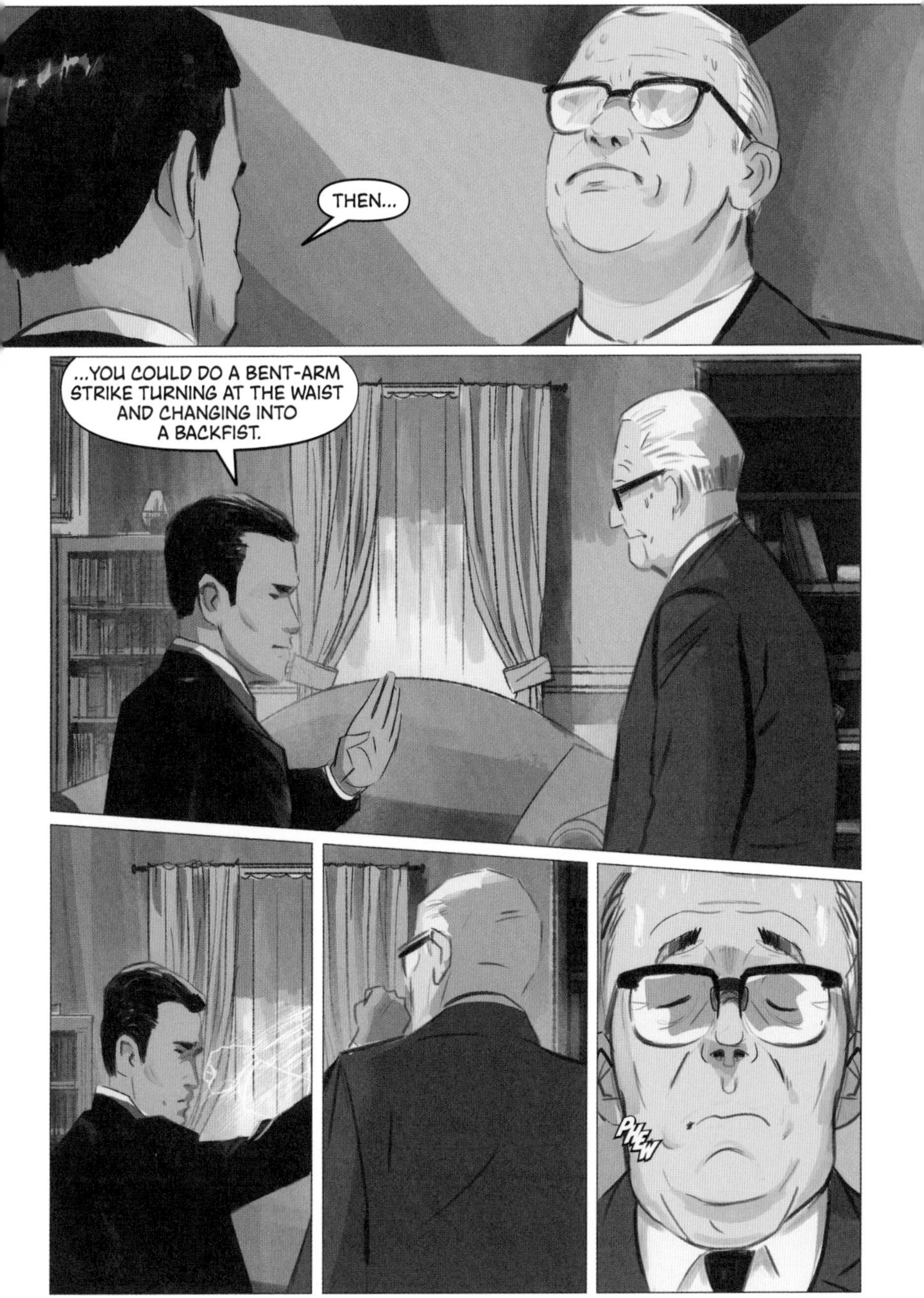
THEN...
...YOU COULD DO A BENT-ARM STRIKE TURNING AT THE WAIST AND CHANGING INTO A BACKFIST.
PHEW

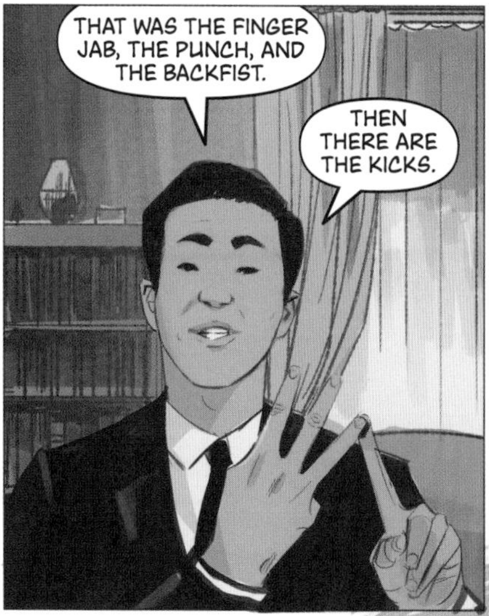
THAT WAS THE FINGER JAB, THE PUNCH, AND THE BACKFIST.
THEN THERE ARE THE KICKS.

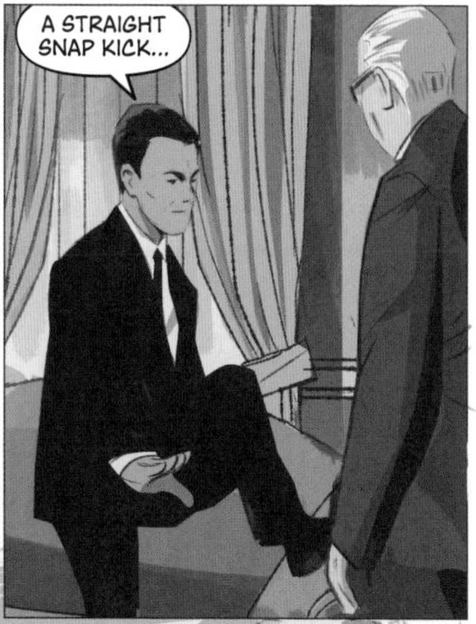
A STRAIGHT SNAP KICK...

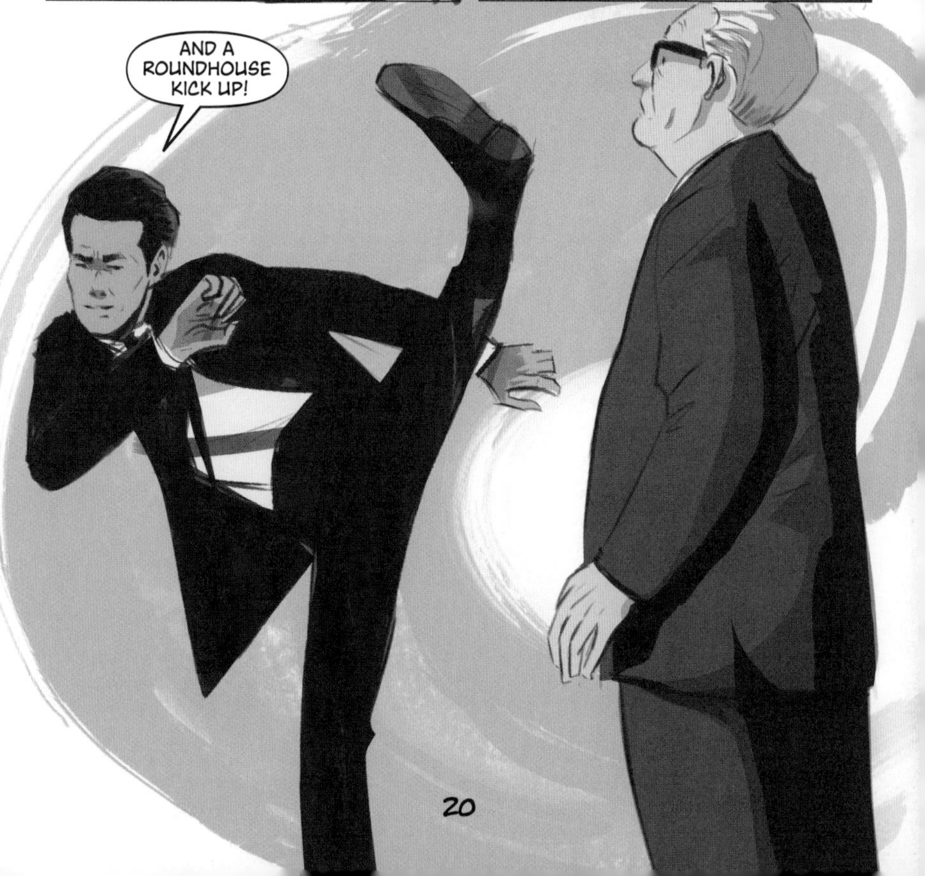
AND A ROUNDHOUSE KICK UP!

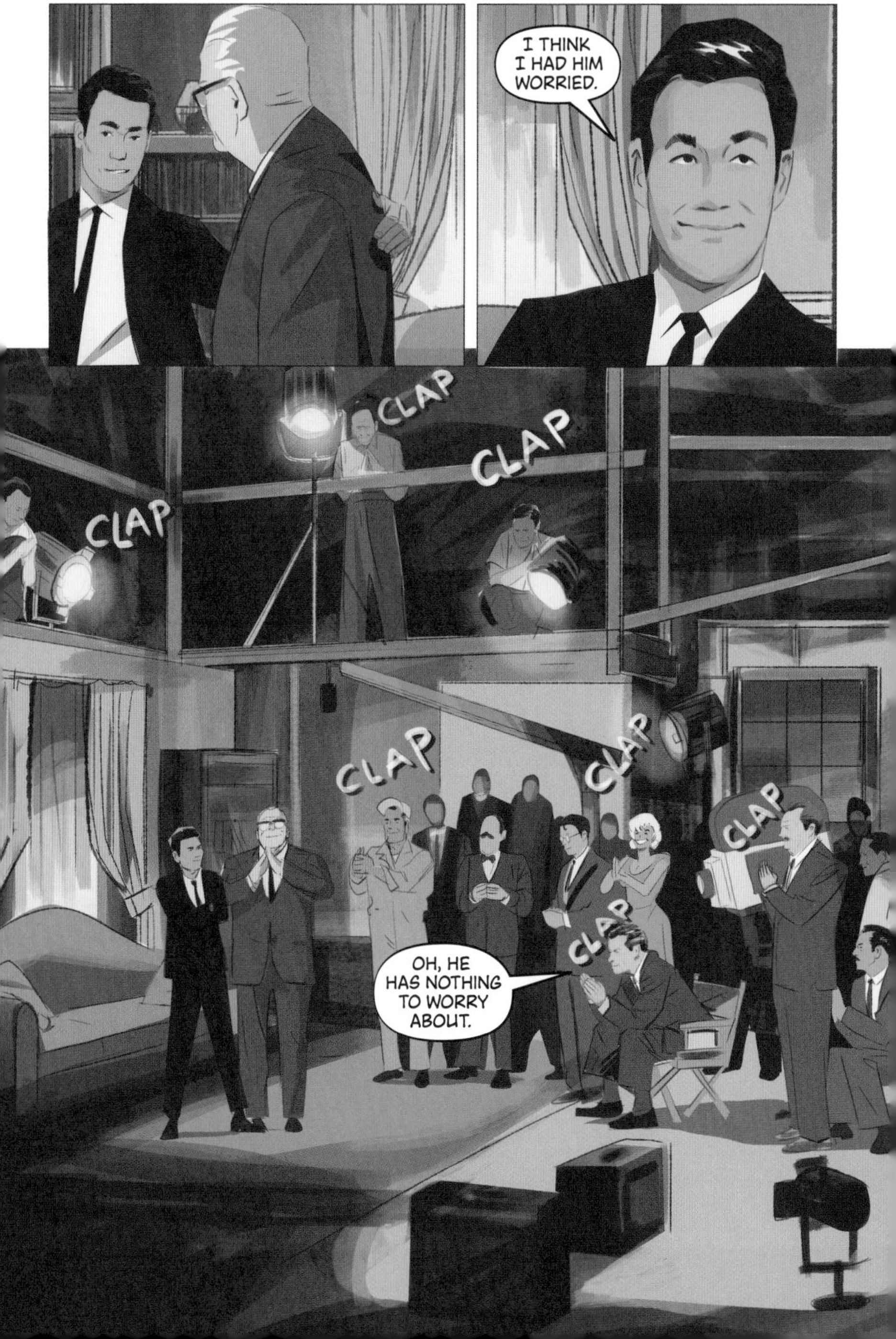
I THINK I HAD HIM WORRIED.
CLAP
CLAP
CLAP
CLAP
CLAP
CLAP
CLAP
OH, HE HAS NOTHING TO WORRY ABOUT.

Gung Fu Fighting

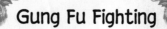

The martial art of gung fu began over three thousand years ago in China.

There are currently hundreds of styles, with most movements imitating the fighting poses of animals and requiring great coordination. The first style that Bruce Lee championed was Wing Chun, which supposedly was created in the 1700s by a Buddhist nun named Ng Mui but named for her disciple Yim Wing Chun. Bruce learned this form from his sifu—his teacher—Ip Man in Hong Kong.

Bruce described gung fu as more fluid, or flowing, than martial arts like karate and jujitsu. He compared this fluidity to water because water is soft and can adjust to any shape it's in, yet it's strong enough to pierce rock. "Be water, my friend" became Bruce's signature phrase.

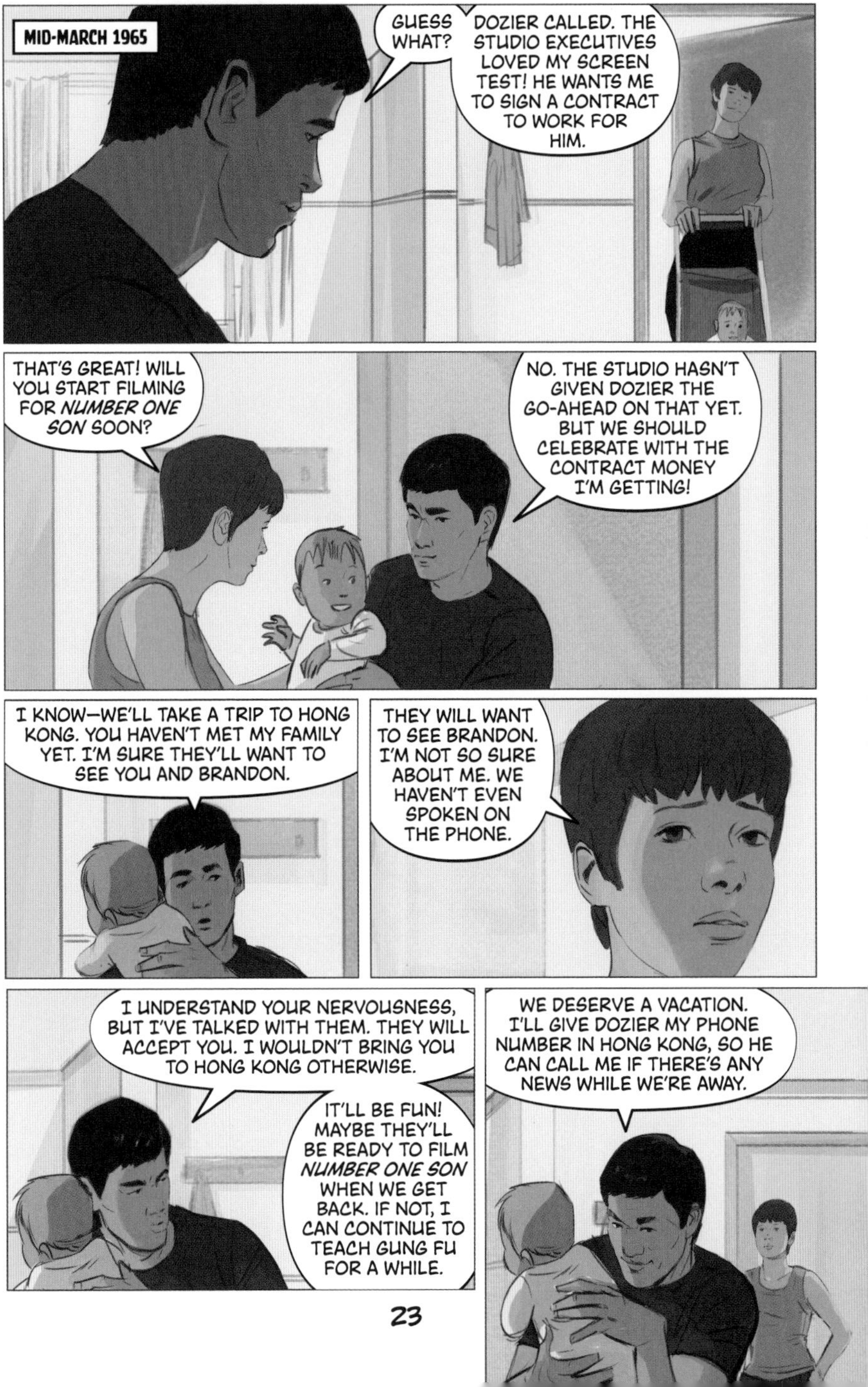
MID-MARCH 1965
GUESS WHAT?
DOZIER CALLED. THE STUDIO EXECUTIVES LOVED MY SCREEN TEST! HE WANTS ME TO SIGN A CONTRACT TO WORK FOR HIM.
THAT'S GREAT! WILL YOU START FILMING FOR *NUMBER ONE SON* SOON?
NO. THE STUDIO HASN'T GIVEN DOZIER THE GO-AHEAD ON THAT YET. BUT WE SHOULD CELEBRATE WITH THE CONTRACT MONEY I'M GETTING!
I KNOW—WE'LL TAKE A TRIP TO HONG KONG. YOU HAVEN'T MET MY FAMILY YET. I'M SURE THEY'LL WANT TO SEE YOU AND BRANDON.
THEY WILL WANT TO SEE BRANDON. I'M NOT SO SURE ABOUT ME. WE HAVEN'T EVEN SPOKEN ON THE PHONE.
I UNDERSTAND YOUR NERVOUSNESS, BUT I'VE TALKED WITH THEM. THEY WILL ACCEPT YOU. I WOULDN'T BRING YOU TO HONG KONG OTHERWISE.
IT'LL BE FUN! MAYBE THEY'LL BE READY TO FILM *NUMBER ONE SON* WHEN WE GET BACK. IF NOT, I CAN CONTINUE TO TEACH GUNG FU FOR A WHILE.
WE DESERVE A VACATION. I'LL GIVE DOZIER MY PHONE NUMBER IN HONG KONG, SO HE CAN CALL ME IF THERE'S ANY NEWS WHILE WE'RE AWAY.

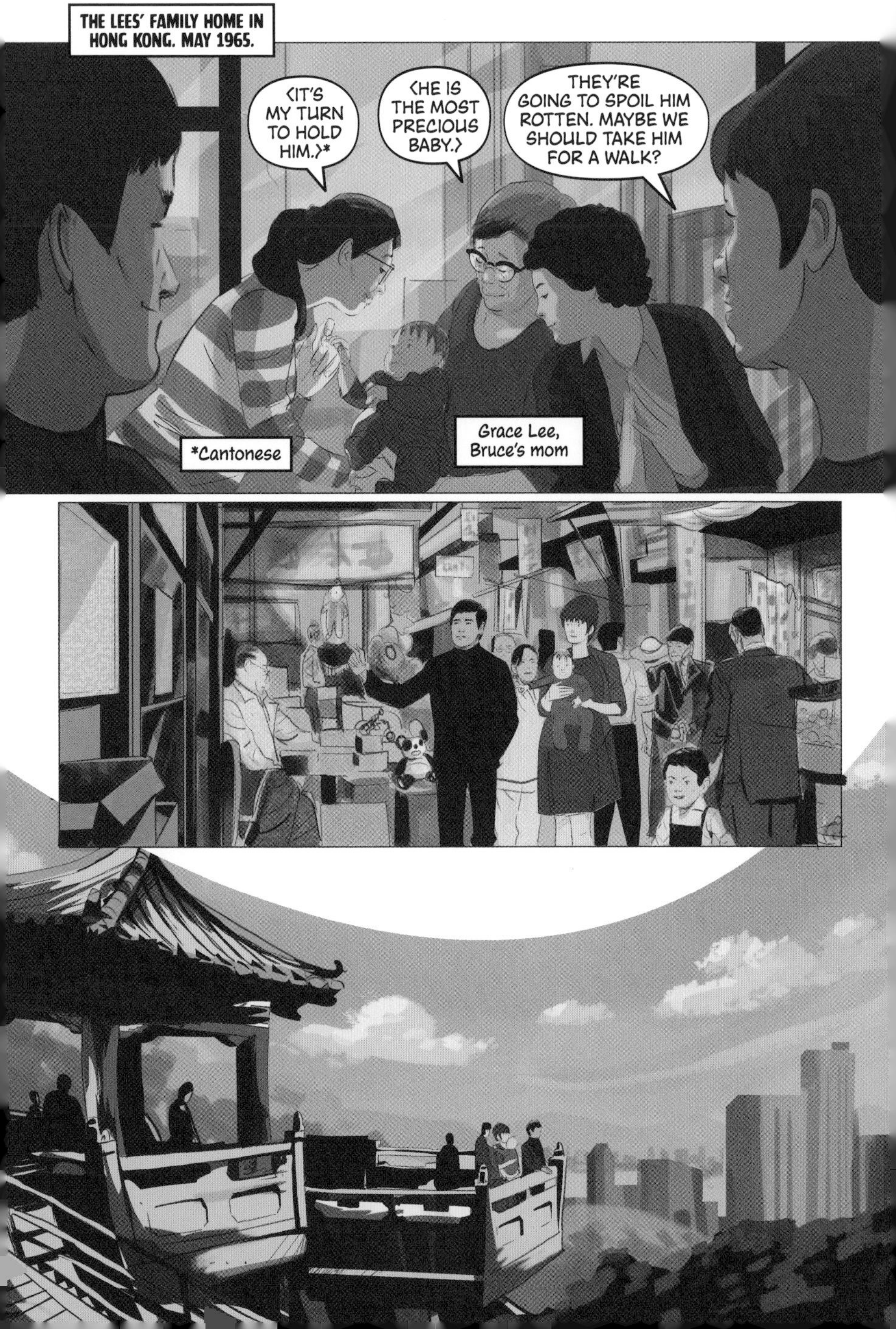
THE LEES' FAMILY HOME IN HONG KONG. MAY 1965.
<IT'S MY TURN TO HOLD HIM.>*
<HE IS THE MOST PRECIOUS BABY.>
THEY'RE GOING TO SPOIL HIM ROTTEN. MAYBE WE SHOULD TAKE HIM FOR A WALK?
Grace Lee, Bruce's mom
*Cantonese

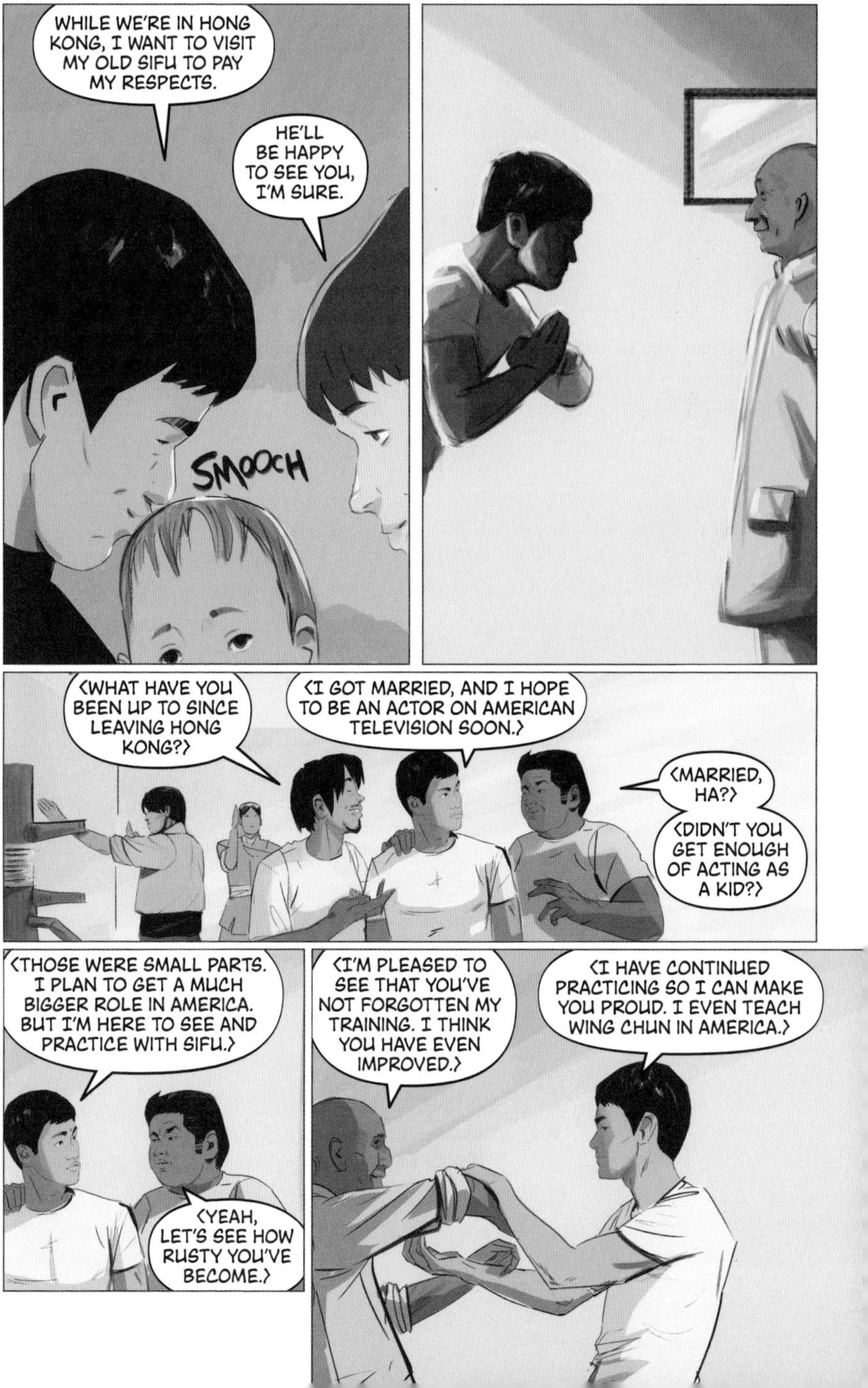
WHILE WE'RE IN HONG KONG, I WANT TO VISIT MY OLD SIFU TO PAY MY RESPECTS.
HE'LL BE HAPPY TO SEE YOU, I'M SURE.
SMOOCH
<WHAT HAVE YOU BEEN UP TO SINCE LEAVING HONG KONG?>
<I GOT MARRIED, AND I HOPE TO BE AN ACTOR ON AMERICAN TELEVISION SOON.>
<MARRIED, HA?>
<DIDN'T YOU GET ENOUGH OF ACTING AS A KID?>
<THOSE WERE SMALL PARTS. I PLAN TO GET A MUCH BIGGER ROLE IN AMERICA. BUT I'M HERE TO SEE AND PRACTICE WITH SIFU.>
<YEAH, LET'S SEE HOW RUSTY YOU'VE BECOME.>
<I'M PLEASED TO SEE THAT YOU'VE NOT FORGOTTEN MY TRAINING. I THINK YOU HAVE EVEN IMPROVED.>
<I HAVE CONTINUED PRACTICING SO I CAN MAKE YOU PROUD. I EVEN TEACH WING CHUN IN AMERICA.>

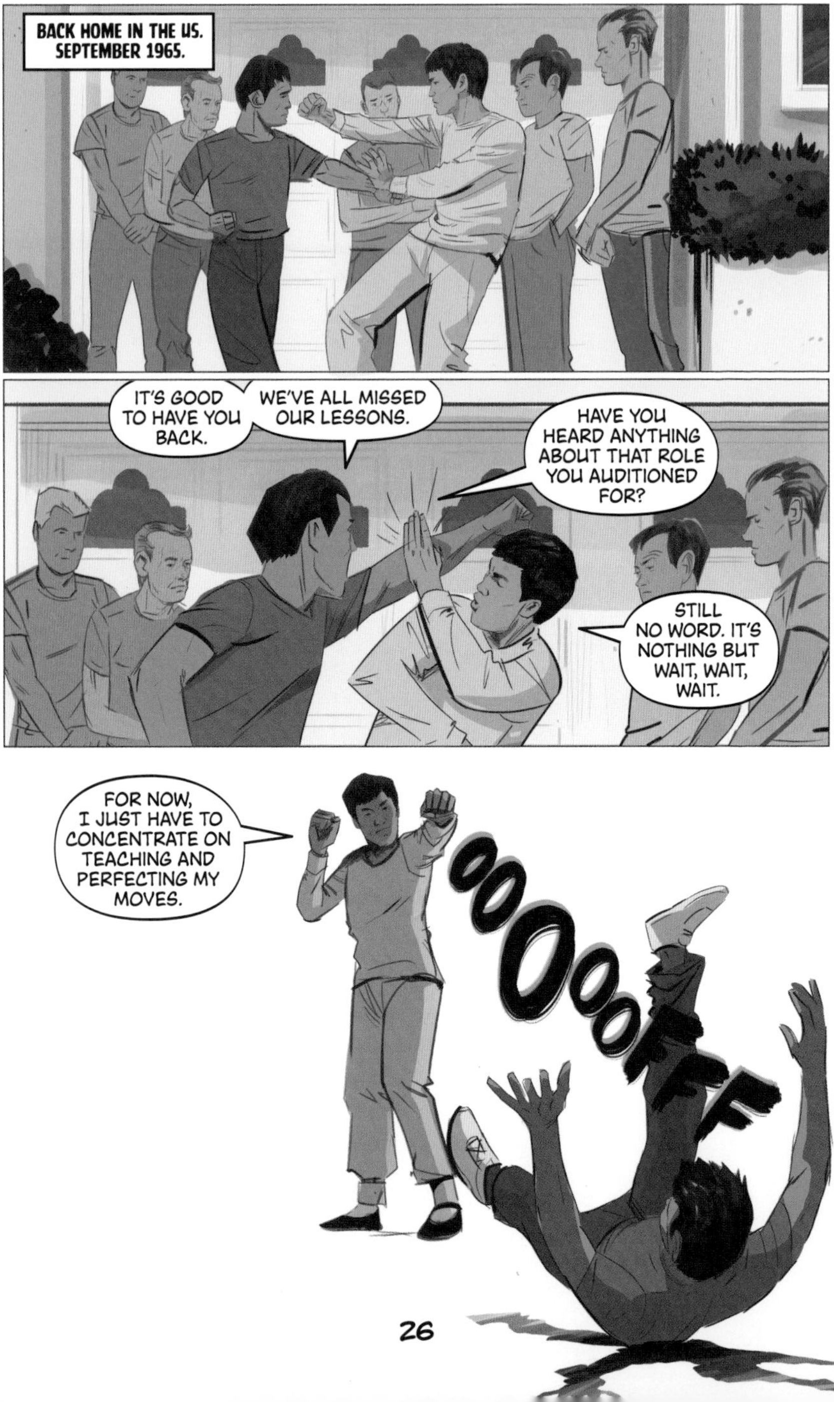
BACK HOME IN THE US. SEPTEMBER 1965.
IT'S GOOD TO HAVE YOU BACK.
WE'VE ALL MISSED OUR LESSONS.
HAVE YOU HEARD ANYTHING ABOUT THAT ROLE YOU AUDITIONED FOR?
STILL NO WORD. IT'S NOTHING BUT WAIT, WAIT, WAIT.
FOR NOW, I JUST HAVE TO CONCENTRATE ON TEACHING AND PERFECTING MY MOVES.
OOOOOOFF

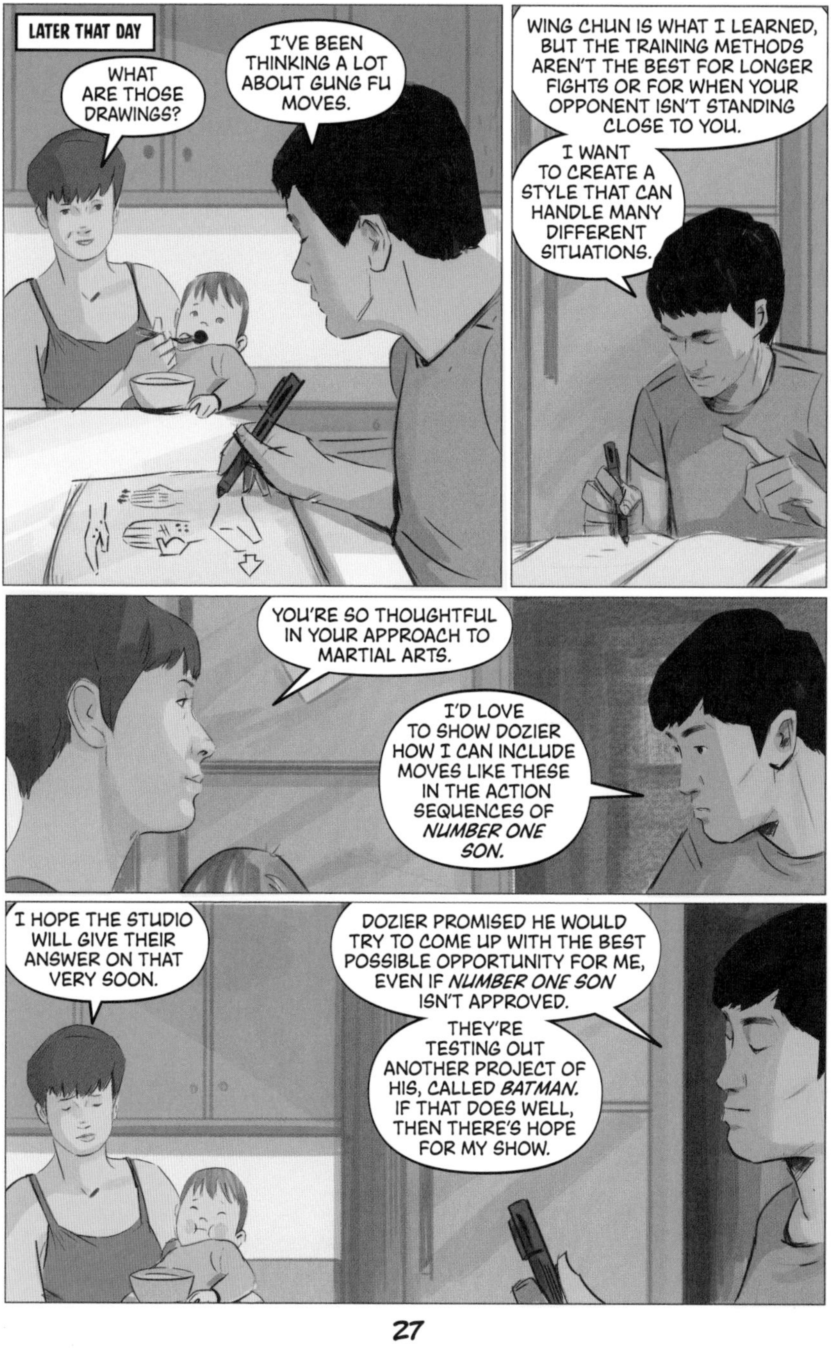
LATER THAT DAY
WHAT ARE THOSE DRAWINGS?
I'VE BEEN THINKING A LOT ABOUT GUNG FU MOVES.
WING CHUN IS WHAT I LEARNED, BUT THE TRAINING METHODS AREN'T THE BEST FOR LONGER FIGHTS OR FOR WHEN YOUR OPPONENT ISN'T STANDING CLOSE TO YOU.
I WANT TO CREATE A STYLE THAT CAN HANDLE MANY DIFFERENT SITUATIONS.
YOU'RE SO THOUGHTFUL IN YOUR APPROACH TO MARTIAL ARTS.
I'D LOVE TO SHOW DOZIER HOW I CAN INCLUDE MOVES LIKE THESE IN THE ACTION SEQUENCES OF *NUMBER ONE SON.*
I HOPE THE STUDIO WILL GIVE THEIR ANSWER ON THAT VERY SOON.
DOZIER PROMISED HE WOULD TRY TO COME UP WITH THE BEST POSSIBLE OPPORTUNITY FOR ME, EVEN IF *NUMBER ONE SON* ISN'T APPROVED.
THEY'RE TESTING OUT ANOTHER PROJECT OF HIS, CALLED *BATMAN.* IF THAT DOES WELL, THEN THERE'S HOPE FOR MY SHOW.

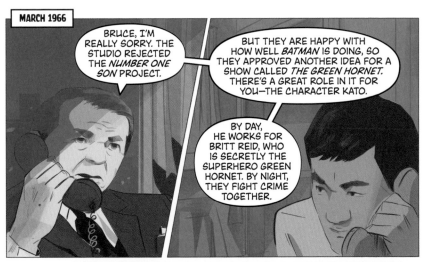

BRUCE, I'M REALLY SORRY. THE STUDIO REJECTED THE *NUMBER ONE SON* PROJECT.

BUT THEY ARE HAPPY WITH HOW WELL *BATMAN* IS DOING, SO THEY APPROVED ANOTHER IDEA FOR A SHOW CALLED *THE GREEN HORNET.* THERE'S A GREAT ROLE IN IT FOR YOU—THE CHARACTER KATO.

BY DAY, HE WORKS FOR BRITT REID, WHO IS SECRETLY THE SUPERHERO GREEN HORNET. BY NIGHT, THEY FIGHT CRIME TOGETHER.

KATO WORKS FOR HIM?

I KNOW WHAT ROLES LIKE THAT MEAN FOR PEOPLE LIKE ME. I AM *NOT* GOING TO PLAY A TYPICAL HOUSEBOY FOR SOME RICH WHITE PERSON.

NO, NO; IT'S NOT LIKE THAT. KATO ISN'T REALLY A SERVANT—HE'S MORE OF A PARTNER TO THE GREEN HORNET.

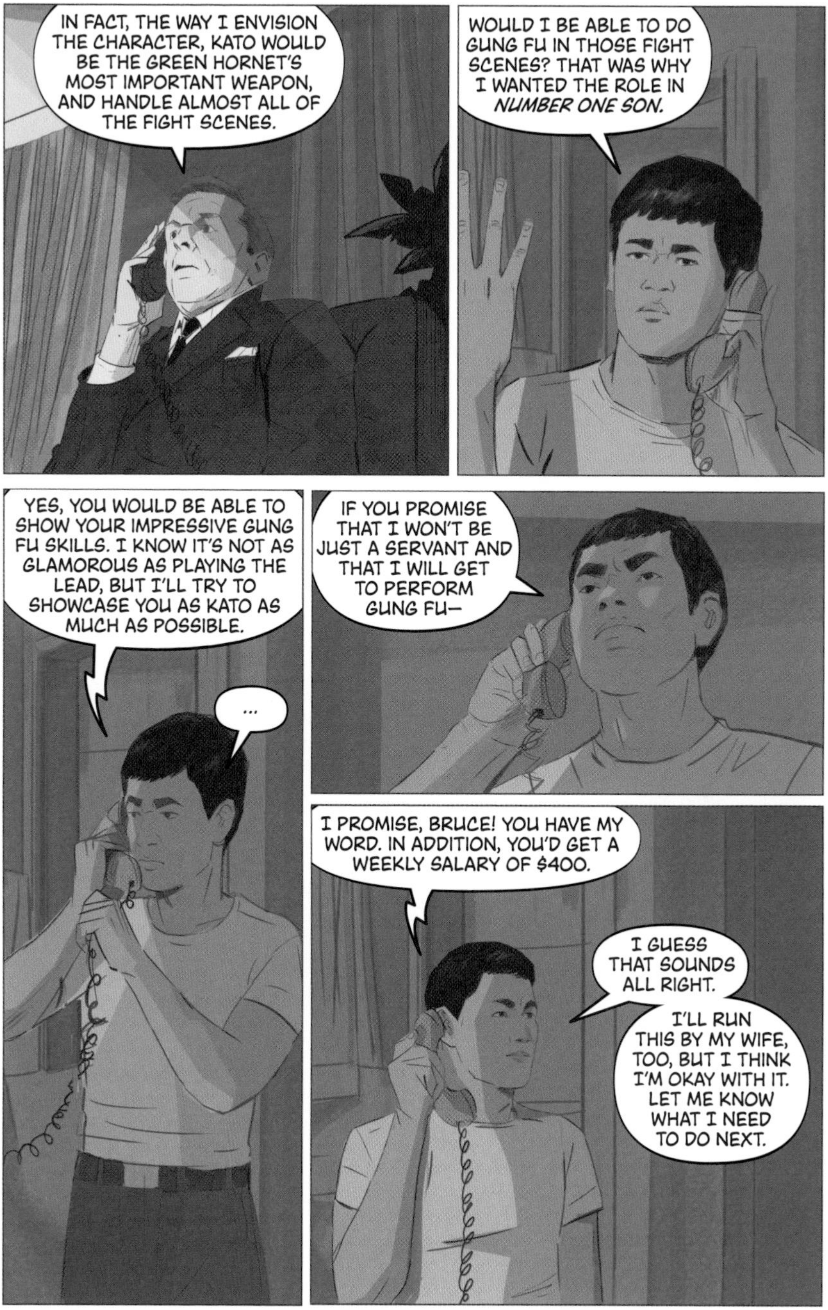
IN FACT, THE WAY I ENVISION THE CHARACTER, KATO WOULD BE THE GREEN HORNET'S MOST IMPORTANT WEAPON, AND HANDLE ALMOST ALL OF THE FIGHT SCENES.
WOULD I BE ABLE TO DO GUNG FU IN THOSE FIGHT SCENES? THAT WAS WHY I WANTED THE ROLE IN *NUMBER ONE SON.*
YES, YOU WOULD BE ABLE TO SHOW YOUR IMPRESSIVE GUNG FU SKILLS. I KNOW IT'S NOT AS GLAMOROUS AS PLAYING THE LEAD, BUT I'LL TRY TO SHOWCASE YOU AS KATO AS MUCH AS POSSIBLE.
...
IF YOU PROMISE THAT I WON'T BE JUST A SERVANT AND THAT I WILL GET TO PERFORM GUNG FU—
I PROMISE, BRUCE! YOU HAVE MY WORD. IN ADDITION, YOU'D GET A WEEKLY SALARY OF $400.
I GUESS THAT SOUNDS ALL RIGHT.
I'LL RUN THIS BY MY WIFE, TOO, BUT I THINK I'M OKAY WITH IT. LET ME KNOW WHAT I NEED TO DO NEXT.

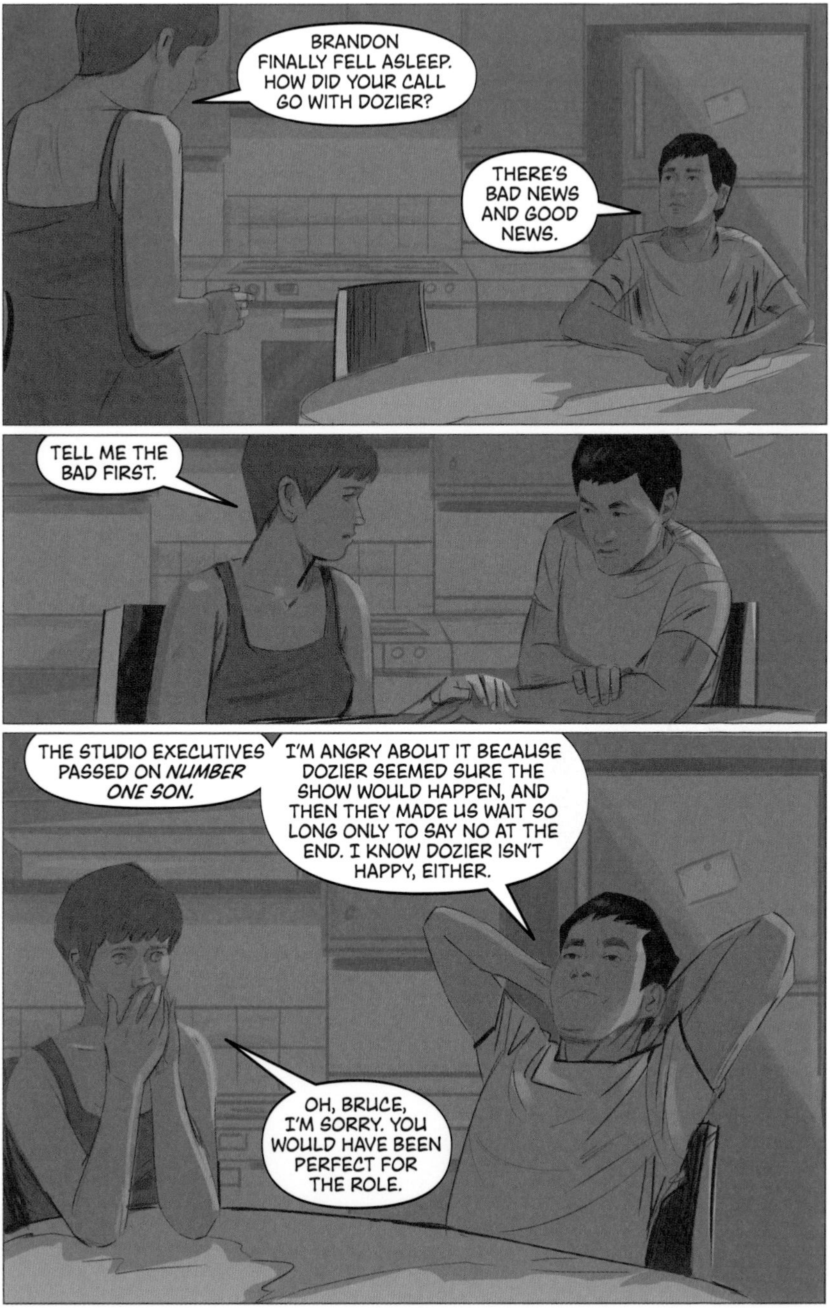
BRANDON FINALLY FELL ASLEEP. HOW DID YOUR CALL GO WITH DOZIER?
THERE'S BAD NEWS AND GOOD NEWS.
TELL ME THE BAD FIRST.
THE STUDIO EXECUTIVES PASSED ON *NUMBER ONE SON.*
I'M ANGRY ABOUT IT BECAUSE DOZIER SEEMED SURE THE SHOW WOULD HAPPEN, AND THEN THEY MADE US WAIT SO LONG ONLY TO SAY NO AT THE END. I KNOW DOZIER ISN'T HAPPY, EITHER.
OH, BRUCE, I'M SORRY. YOU WOULD HAVE BEEN PERFECT FOR THE ROLE.

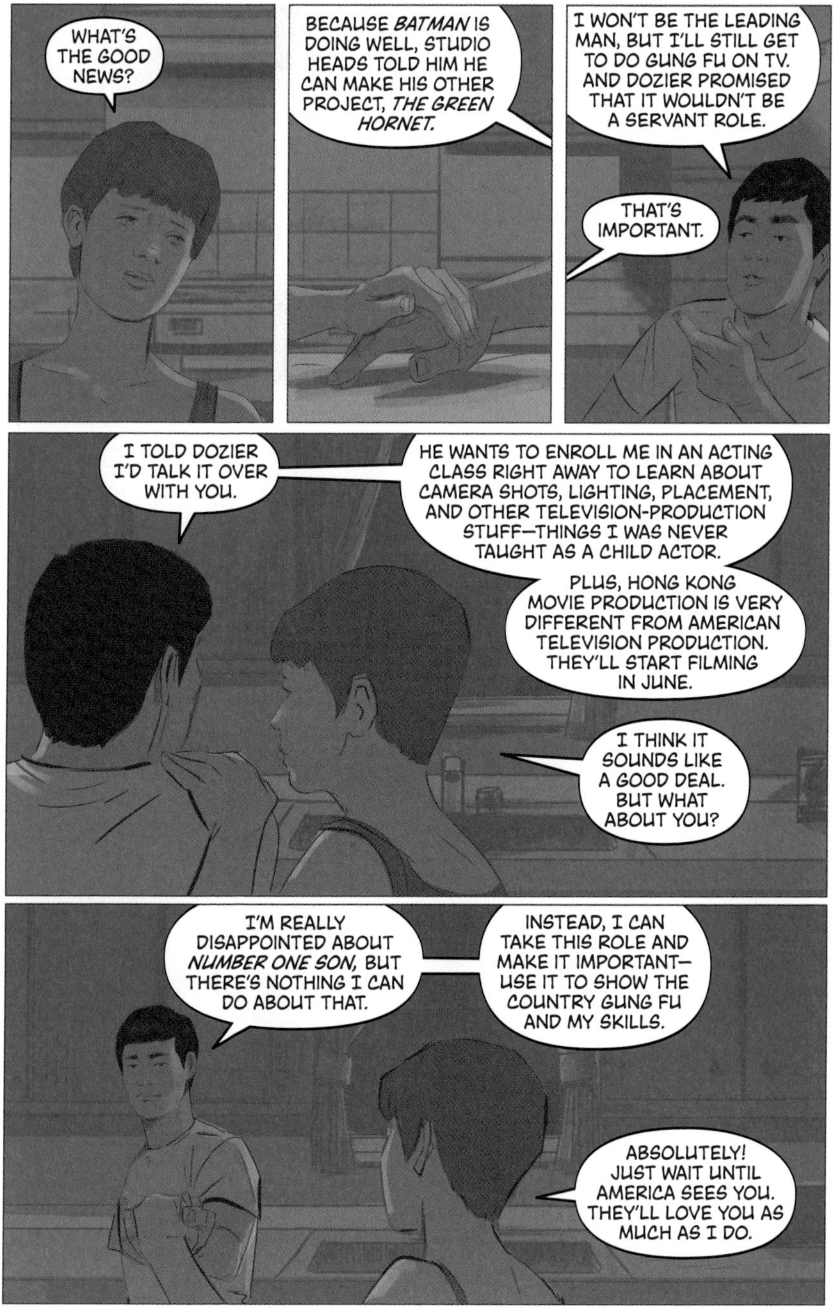
WHAT'S THE GOOD NEWS?
BECAUSE *BATMAN* IS DOING WELL, STUDIO HEADS TOLD HIM HE CAN MAKE HIS OTHER PROJECT, *THE GREEN HORNET.*
I WON'T BE THE LEADING MAN, BUT I'LL STILL GET TO DO GUNG FU ON TV. AND DOZIER PROMISED THAT IT WOULDN'T BE A SERVANT ROLE.
THAT'S IMPORTANT.
I TOLD DOZIER I'D TALK IT OVER WITH YOU.
HE WANTS TO ENROLL ME IN AN ACTING CLASS RIGHT AWAY TO LEARN ABOUT CAMERA SHOTS, LIGHTING, PLACEMENT, AND OTHER TELEVISION-PRODUCTION STUFF—THINGS I WAS NEVER TAUGHT AS A CHILD ACTOR.
PLUS, HONG KONG MOVIE PRODUCTION IS VERY DIFFERENT FROM AMERICAN TELEVISION PRODUCTION. THEY'LL START FILMING IN JUNE.
I THINK IT SOUNDS LIKE A GOOD DEAL. BUT WHAT ABOUT YOU?
I'M REALLY DISAPPOINTED ABOUT *NUMBER ONE SON,* BUT THERE'S NOTHING I CAN DO ABOUT THAT.
INSTEAD, I CAN TAKE THIS ROLE AND MAKE IT IMPORTANT—USE IT TO SHOW THE COUNTRY GUNG FU AND MY SKILLS.
ABSOLUTELY! JUST WAIT UNTIL AMERICA SEES YOU. THEY'LL LOVE YOU AS MUCH AS I DO.

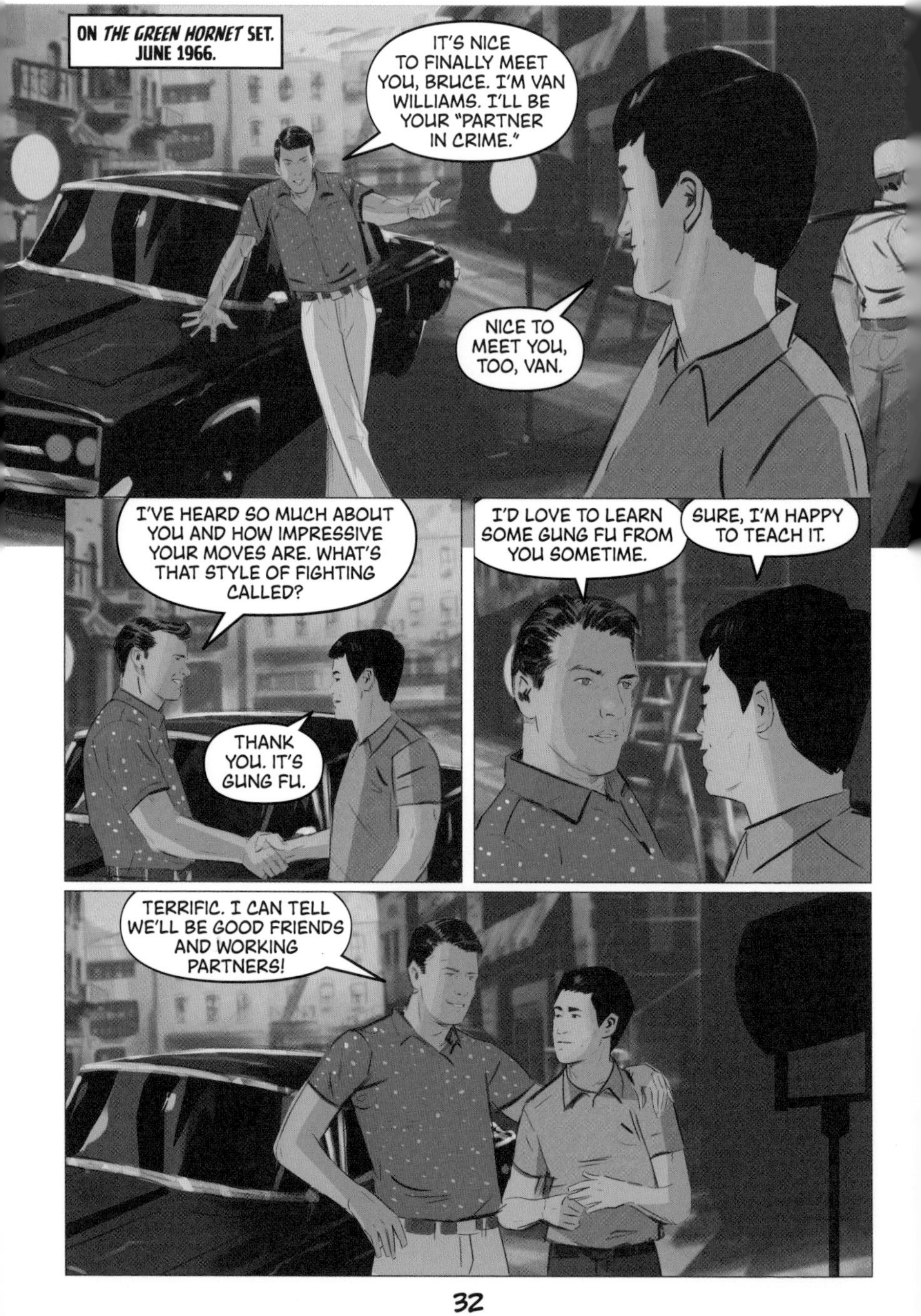
ON THE GREEN HORNET SET. JUNE 1966.
IT'S NICE TO FINALLY MEET YOU, BRUCE. I'M VAN WILLIAMS. I'LL BE YOUR "PARTNER IN CRIME."
NICE TO MEET YOU, TOO, VAN.
I'VE HEARD SO MUCH ABOUT YOU AND HOW IMPRESSIVE YOUR MOVES ARE. WHAT'S THAT STYLE OF FIGHTING CALLED?
THANK YOU. IT'S GUNG FU.
I'D LOVE TO LEARN SOME GUNG FU FROM YOU SOMETIME.
SURE, I'M HAPPY TO TEACH IT.
TERRIFIC. I CAN TELL WE'LL BE GOOD FRIENDS AND WORKING PARTNERS!

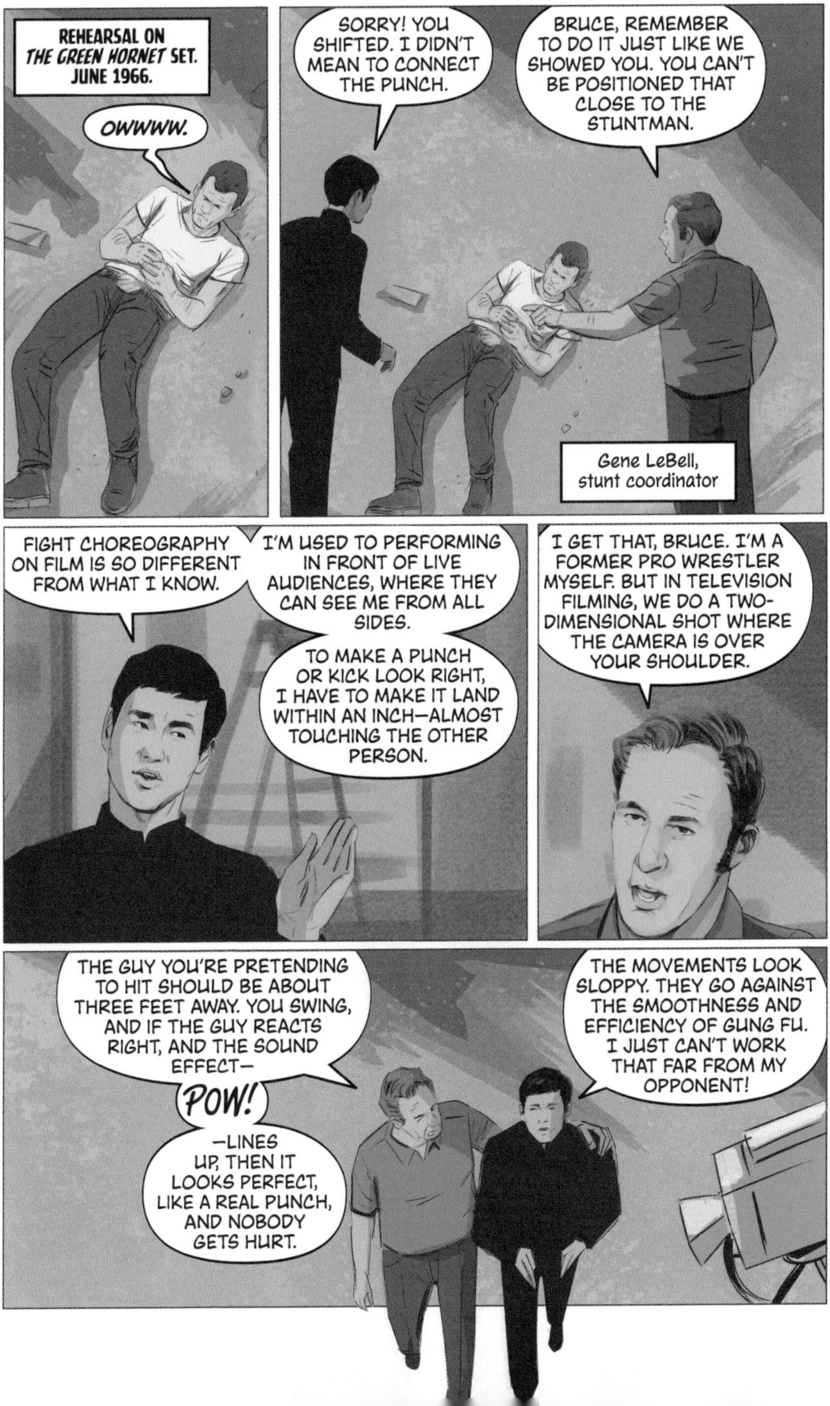
REHEARSAL ON *THE GREEN HORNET* SET. JUNE 1966.
OWWWW.
SORRY! YOU SHIFTED. I DIDN'T MEAN TO CONNECT THE PUNCH.
BRUCE, REMEMBER TO DO IT JUST LIKE WE SHOWED YOU. YOU CAN'T BE POSITIONED THAT CLOSE TO THE STUNTMAN.
Gene LeBell, stunt coordinator
FIGHT CHOREOGRAPHY ON FILM IS SO DIFFERENT FROM WHAT I KNOW.
I'M USED TO PERFORMING IN FRONT OF LIVE AUDIENCES, WHERE THEY CAN SEE ME FROM ALL SIDES.
TO MAKE A PUNCH OR KICK LOOK RIGHT, I HAVE TO MAKE IT LAND WITHIN AN INCH—ALMOST TOUCHING THE OTHER PERSON.
I GET THAT, BRUCE. I'M A FORMER PRO WRESTLER MYSELF. BUT IN TELEVISION FILMING, WE DO A TWO-DIMENSIONAL SHOT WHERE THE CAMERA IS OVER YOUR SHOULDER.
THE GUY YOU'RE PRETENDING TO HIT SHOULD BE ABOUT THREE FEET AWAY. YOU SWING, AND IF THE GUY REACTS RIGHT, AND THE SOUND EFFECT—
POW!
—LINES UP, THEN IT LOOKS PERFECT, LIKE A REAL PUNCH, AND NOBODY GETS HURT.
THE MOVEMENTS LOOK SLOPPY. THEY GO AGAINST THE SMOOTHNESS AND EFFICIENCY OF GUNG FU. I JUST CAN'T WORK THAT FAR FROM MY OPPONENT!

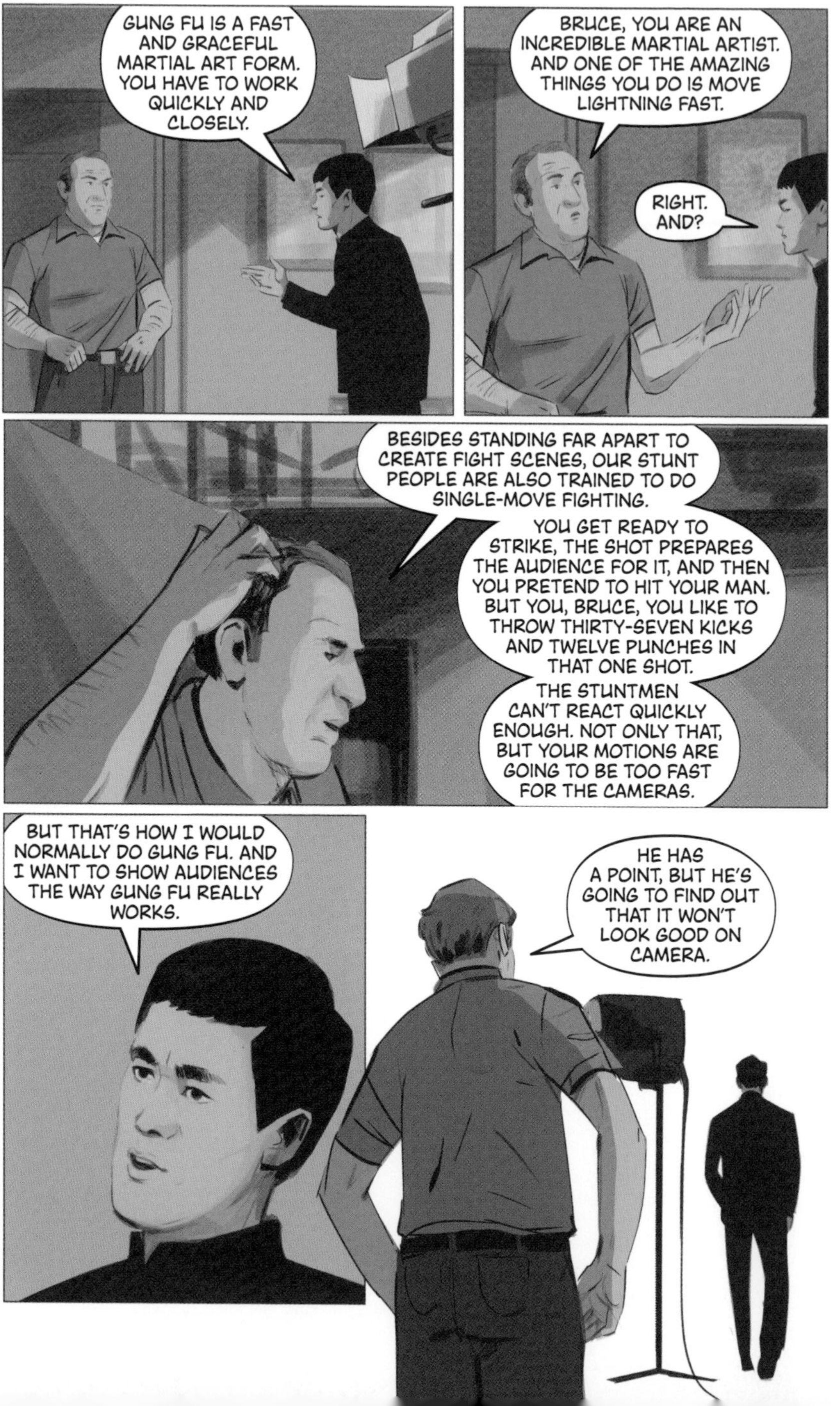
GUNG FU IS A FAST AND GRACEFUL MARTIAL ART FORM. YOU HAVE TO WORK QUICKLY AND CLOSELY.
BRUCE, YOU ARE AN INCREDIBLE MARTIAL ARTIST. AND ONE OF THE AMAZING THINGS YOU DO IS MOVE LIGHTNING FAST.
RIGHT. AND?
BESIDES STANDING FAR APART TO CREATE FIGHT SCENES, OUR STUNT PEOPLE ARE ALSO TRAINED TO DO SINGLE-MOVE FIGHTING.
YOU GET READY TO STRIKE, THE SHOT PREPARES THE AUDIENCE FOR IT, AND THEN YOU PRETEND TO HIT YOUR MAN. BUT YOU, BRUCE, YOU LIKE TO THROW THIRTY-SEVEN KICKS AND TWELVE PUNCHES IN THAT ONE SHOT.
THE STUNTMEN CAN'T REACT QUICKLY ENOUGH. NOT ONLY THAT, BUT YOUR MOTIONS ARE GOING TO BE TOO FAST FOR THE CAMERAS.
BUT THAT'S HOW I WOULD NORMALLY DO GUNG FU. AND I WANT TO SHOW AUDIENCES THE WAY GUNG FU REALLY WORKS.
HE HAS A POINT, BUT HE'S GOING TO FIND OUT THAT IT WON'T LOOK GOOD ON CAMERA.

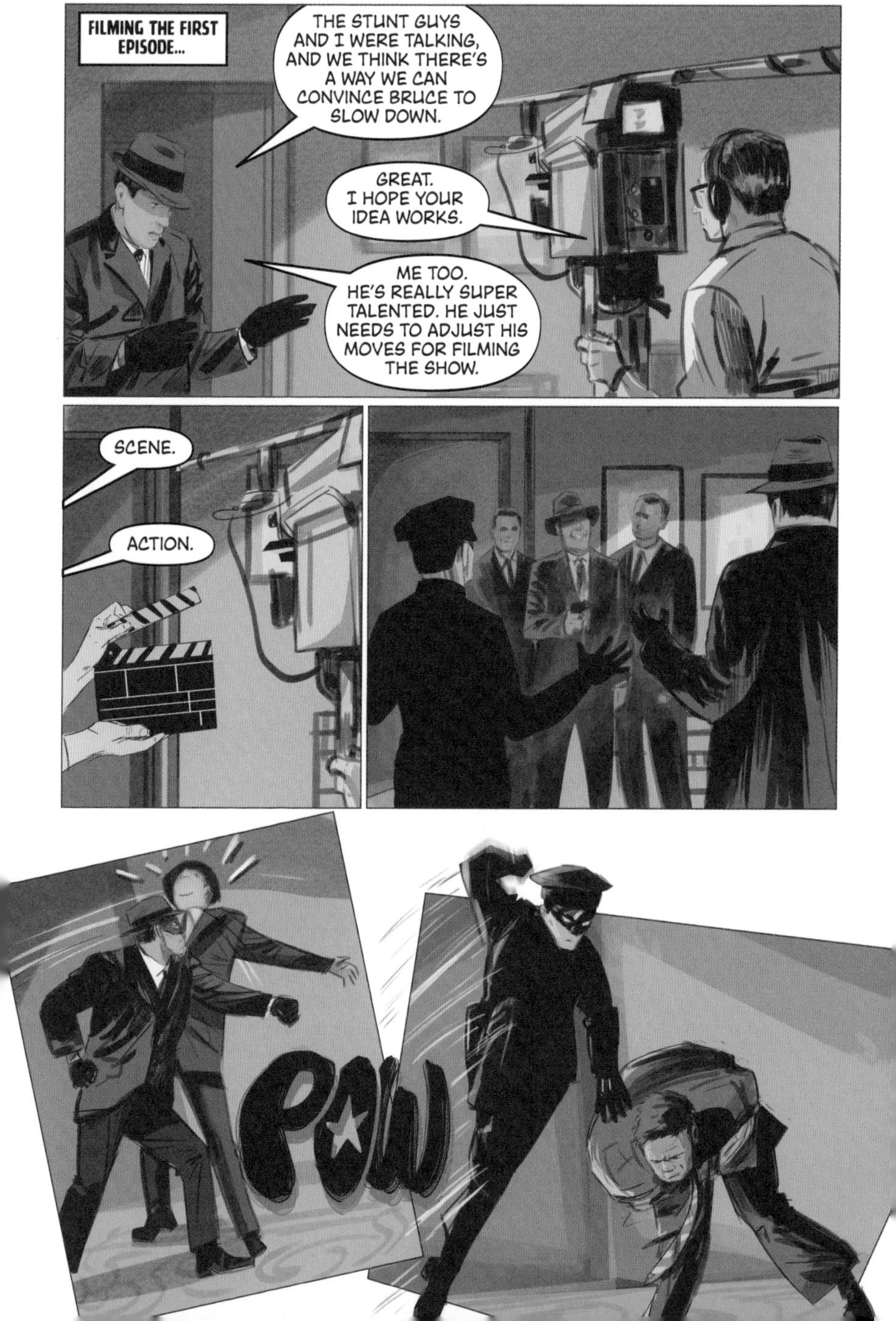
FILMING THE FIRST EPISODE...
THE STUNT GUYS AND I WERE TALKING, AND WE THINK THERE'S A WAY WE CAN CONVINCE BRUCE TO SLOW DOWN.
GREAT. I HOPE YOUR IDEA WORKS.
ME TOO. HE'S REALLY SUPER TALENTED. HE JUST NEEDS TO ADJUST HIS MOVES FOR FILMING THE SHOW.
SCENE.
ACTION.
POW

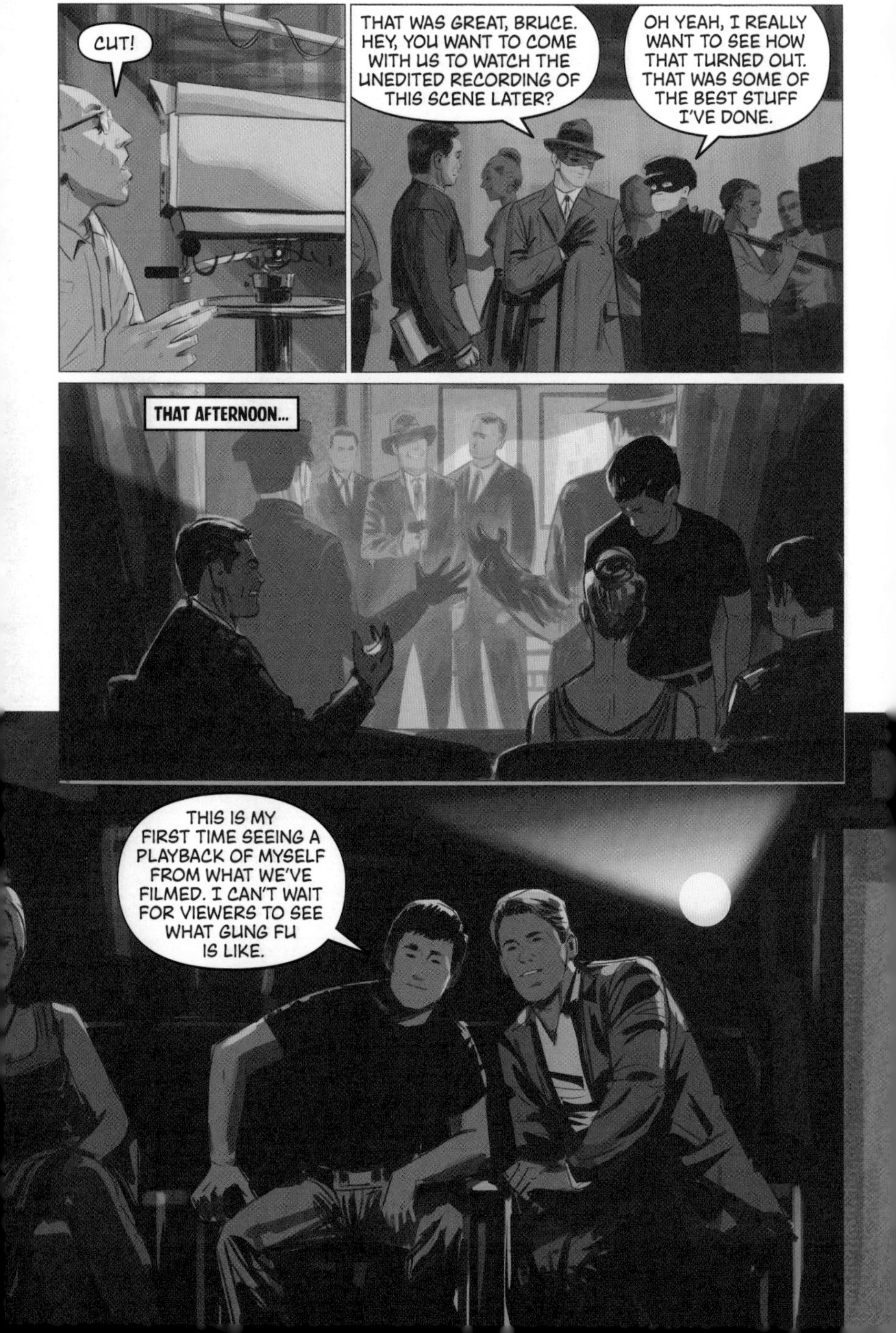
CUT!
THAT WAS GREAT, BRUCE. HEY, YOU WANT TO COME WITH US TO WATCH THE UNEDITED RECORDING OF THIS SCENE LATER?
OH YEAH, I REALLY WANT TO SEE HOW THAT TURNED OUT. THAT WAS SOME OF THE BEST STUFF I'VE DONE.
THAT AFTERNOON...
THIS IS MY FIRST TIME SEEING A PLAYBACK OF MYSELF FROM WHAT WE'VE FILMED. I CAN'T WAIT FOR VIEWERS TO SEE WHAT GUNG FU IS LIKE.

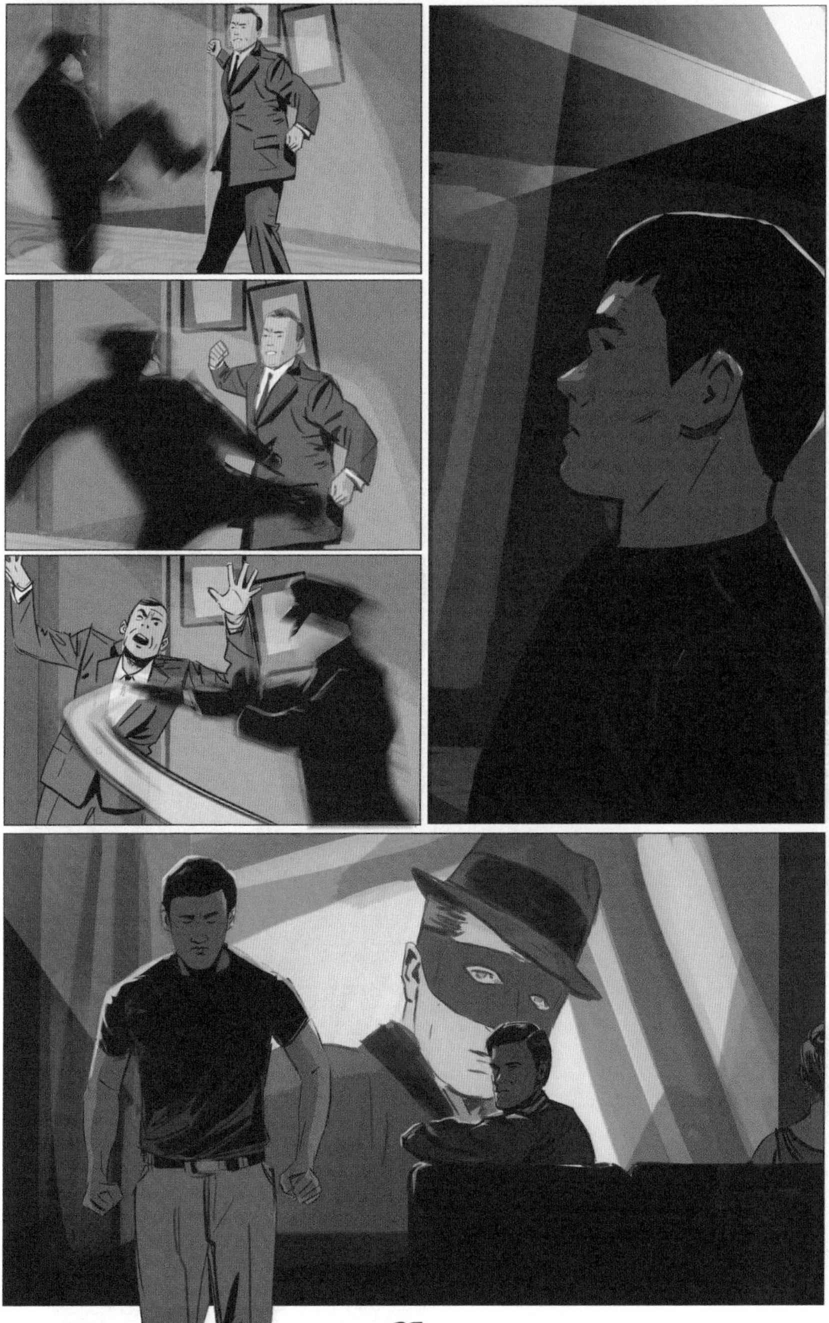

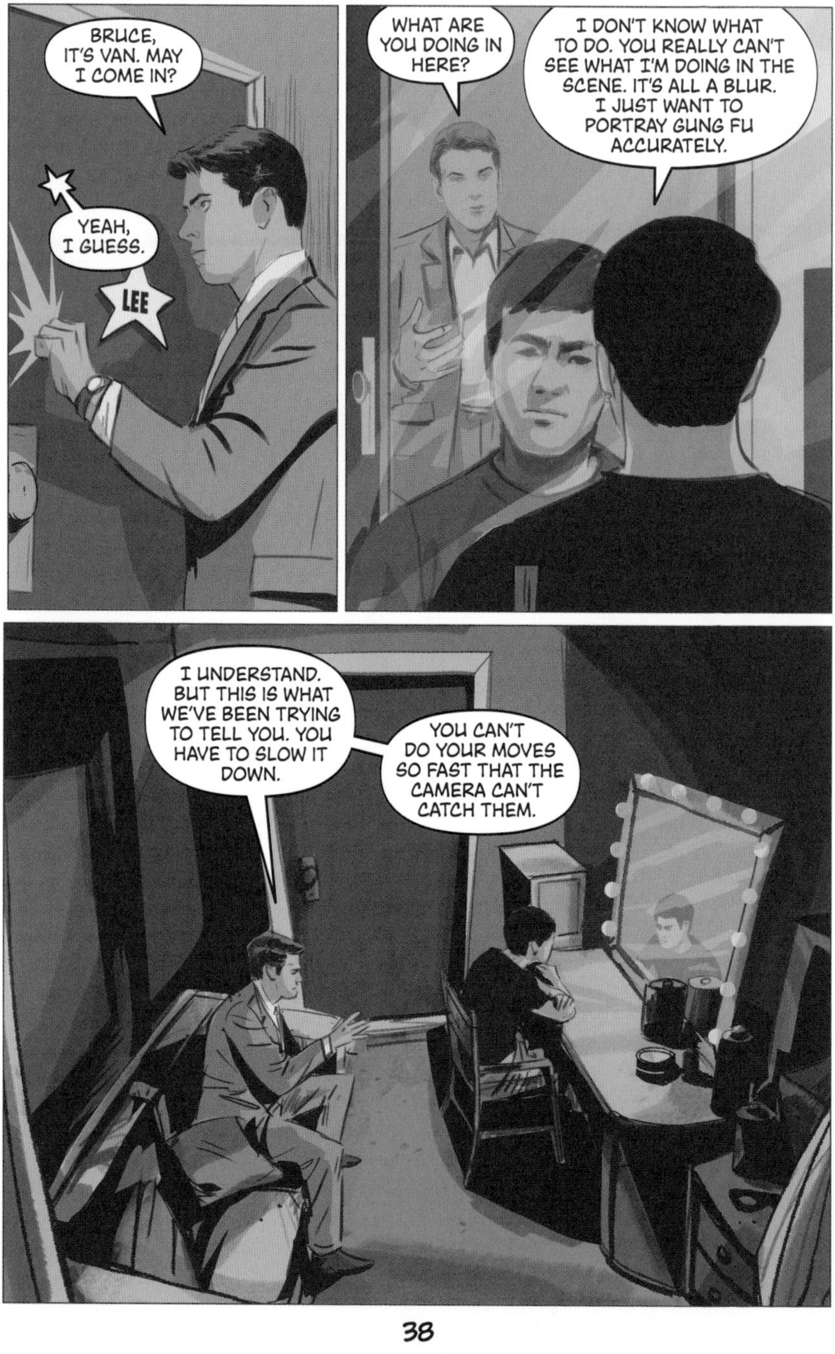
BRUCE, IT'S VAN. MAY I COME IN?
YEAH, I GUESS.
LEE
WHAT ARE YOU DOING IN HERE?
I DON'T KNOW WHAT TO DO. YOU REALLY CAN'T SEE WHAT I'M DOING IN THE SCENE. IT'S ALL A BLUR. I JUST WANT TO PORTRAY GUNG FU ACCURATELY.
I UNDERSTAND. BUT THIS IS WHAT WE'VE BEEN TRYING TO TELL YOU. YOU HAVE TO SLOW IT DOWN.
YOU CAN'T DO YOUR MOVES SO FAST THAT THE CAMERA CAN'T CATCH THEM.

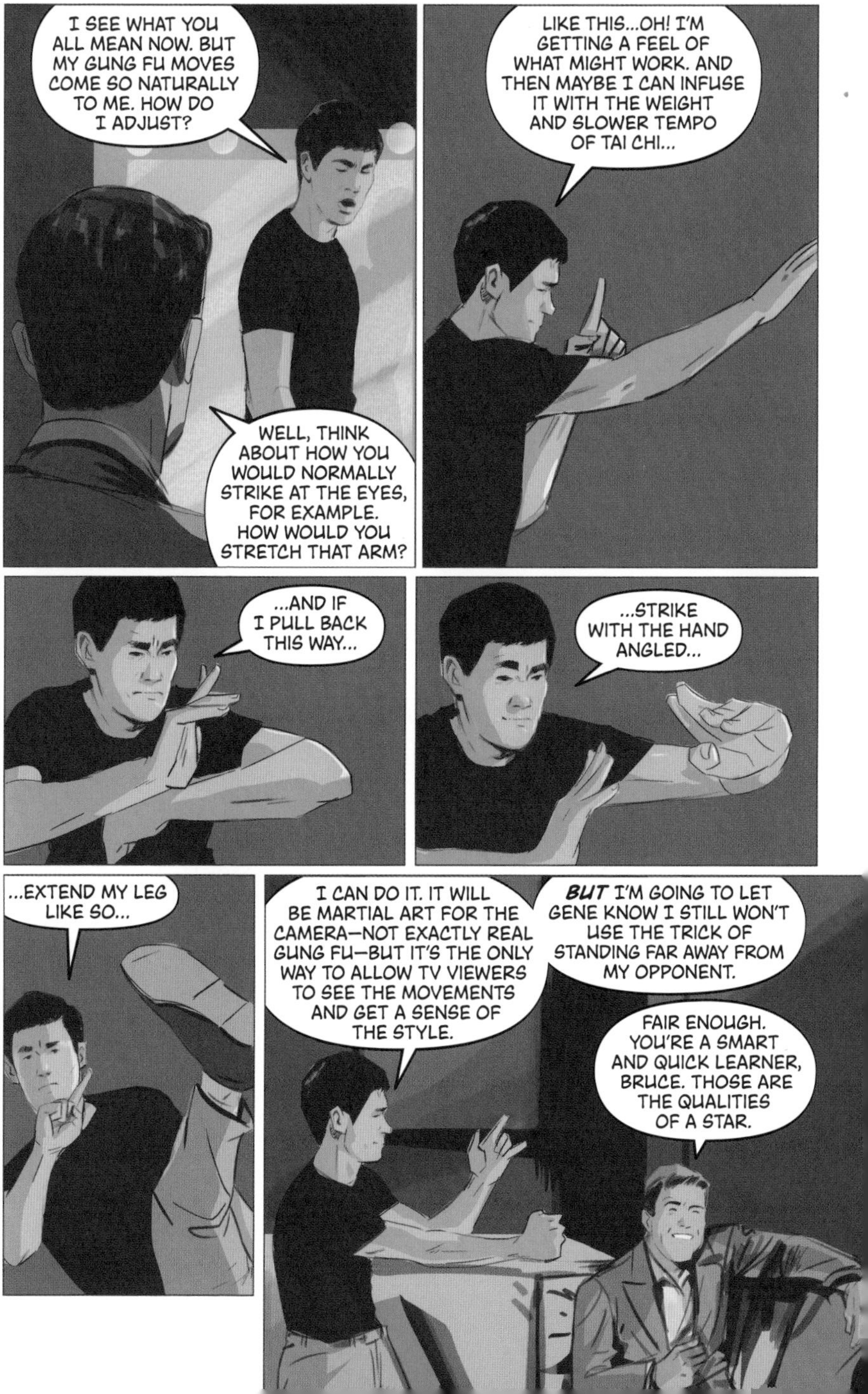
I SEE WHAT YOU ALL MEAN NOW. BUT MY GUNG FU MOVES COME SO NATURALLY TO ME. HOW DO I ADJUST?
WELL, THINK ABOUT HOW YOU WOULD NORMALLY STRIKE AT THE EYES, FOR EXAMPLE. HOW WOULD YOU STRETCH THAT ARM?
LIKE THIS...OH! I'M GETTING A FEEL OF WHAT MIGHT WORK. AND THEN MAYBE I CAN INFUSE IT WITH THE WEIGHT AND SLOWER TEMPO OF TAI CHI...
...AND IF I PULL BACK THIS WAY...
...STRIKE WITH THE HAND ANGLED...
...EXTEND MY LEG LIKE SO...
I CAN DO IT. IT WILL BE MARTIAL ART FOR THE CAMERA—NOT EXACTLY REAL GUNG FU—BUT IT'S THE ONLY WAY TO ALLOW TV VIEWERS TO SEE THE MOVEMENTS AND GET A SENSE OF THE STYLE.
BUT I'M GOING TO LET GENE KNOW I STILL WON'T USE THE TRICK OF STANDING FAR AWAY FROM MY OPPONENT.
FAIR ENOUGH. YOU'RE A SMART AND QUICK LEARNER, BRUCE. THOSE ARE THE QUALITIES OF A STAR.

Kato Kicks Butt

Created by writer George W. Trendle, Kato started as a character on the radio program *The Green Hornet*, which first aired in 1936.

Just as Batman has Robin, the Green Hornet has Kato. With secret identities as a newspaper publisher and his valet, the two become masked crime fighters by night.

Trendle wrote Kato as Japanese, but when Bruce Lee took the role for television, the character was changed to be an unspecified "Asian" ethnicity.

As Kato, Bruce introduced gung fu to American television audiences for the very first time. Initially, Bruce's martial arts moves were too fast to be captured on camera, but after consulting with experienced actors, he adjusted his moves for the screen. However, he refused to follow the clunky Hollywood trick of using camera angles to fake punches and was able to influence fight choreography on *The Green Hornet*. The result was fight scenes that looked exciting and realistic, creating many fans for Bruce and gung fu.

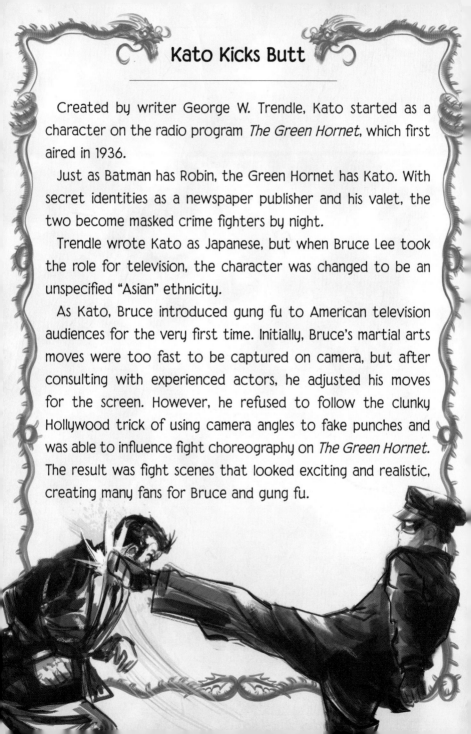

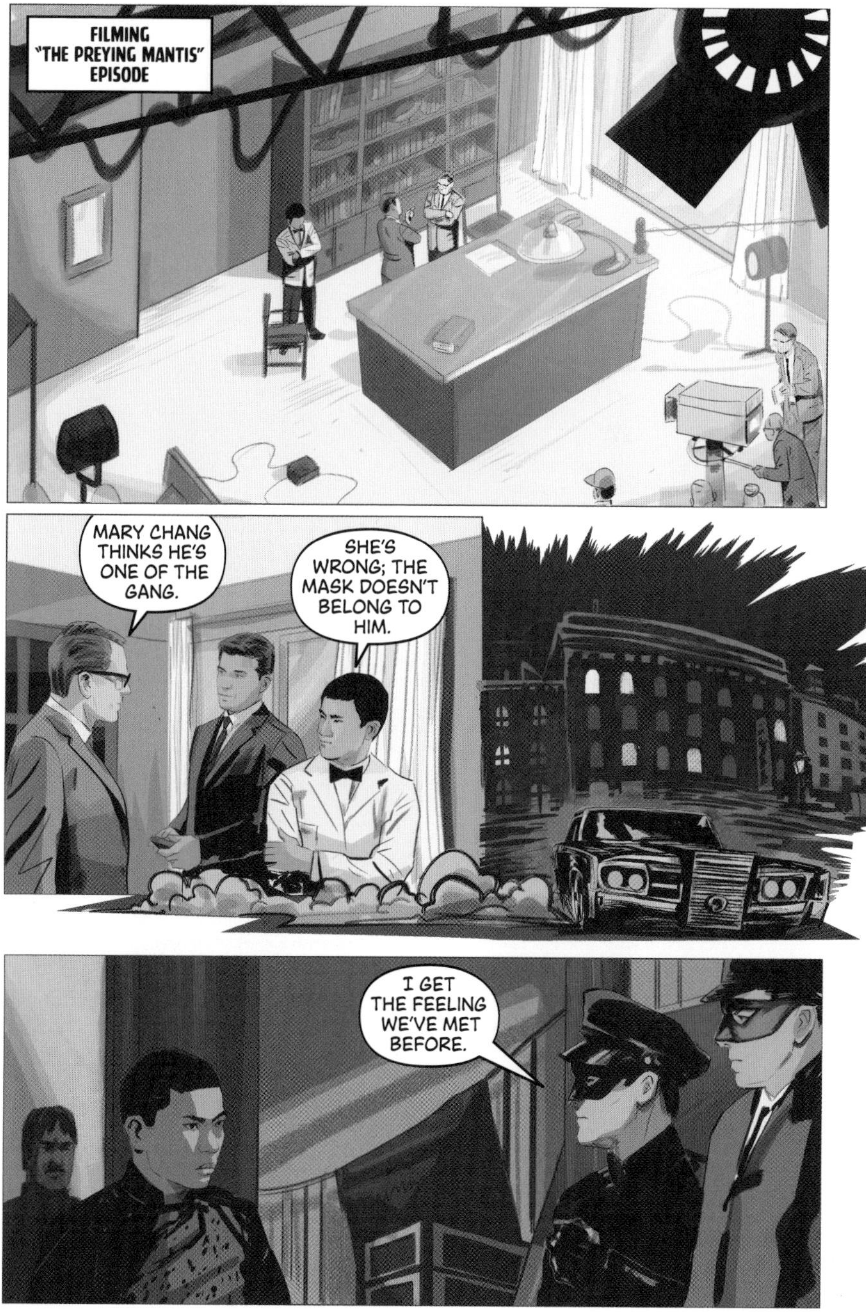
FILMING "THE PREYING MANTIS" EPISODE
MARY CHANG THINKS HE'S ONE OF THE GANG.
SHE'S WRONG; THE MASK DOESN'T BELONG TO HIM.
I GET THE FEELING WE'VE MET BEFORE.

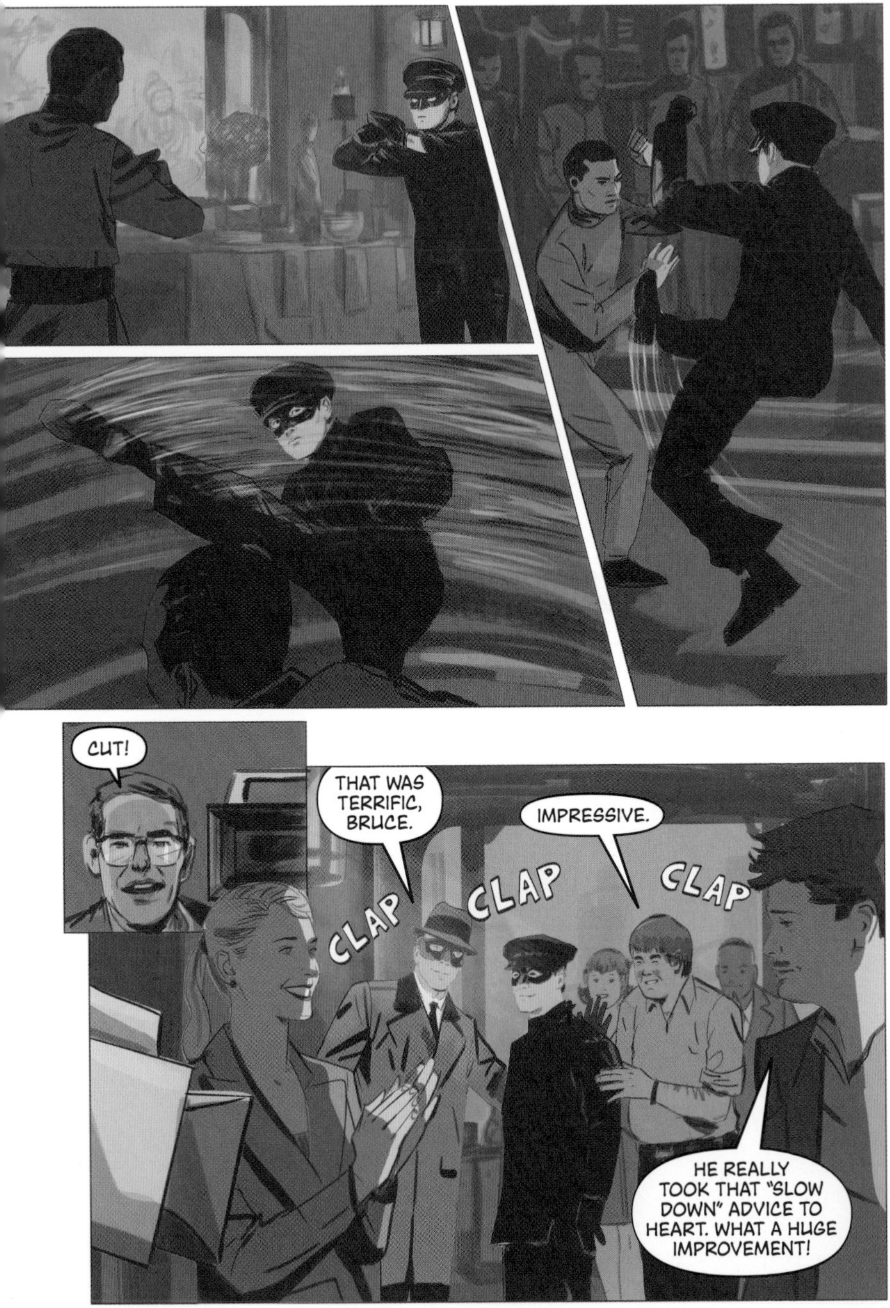
CUT!
THAT WAS TERRIFIC, BRUCE.
CLAP
CLAP
IMPRESSIVE.
CLAP
HE REALLY TOOK THAT "SLOW DOWN" ADVICE TO HEART. WHAT A HUGE IMPROVEMENT!

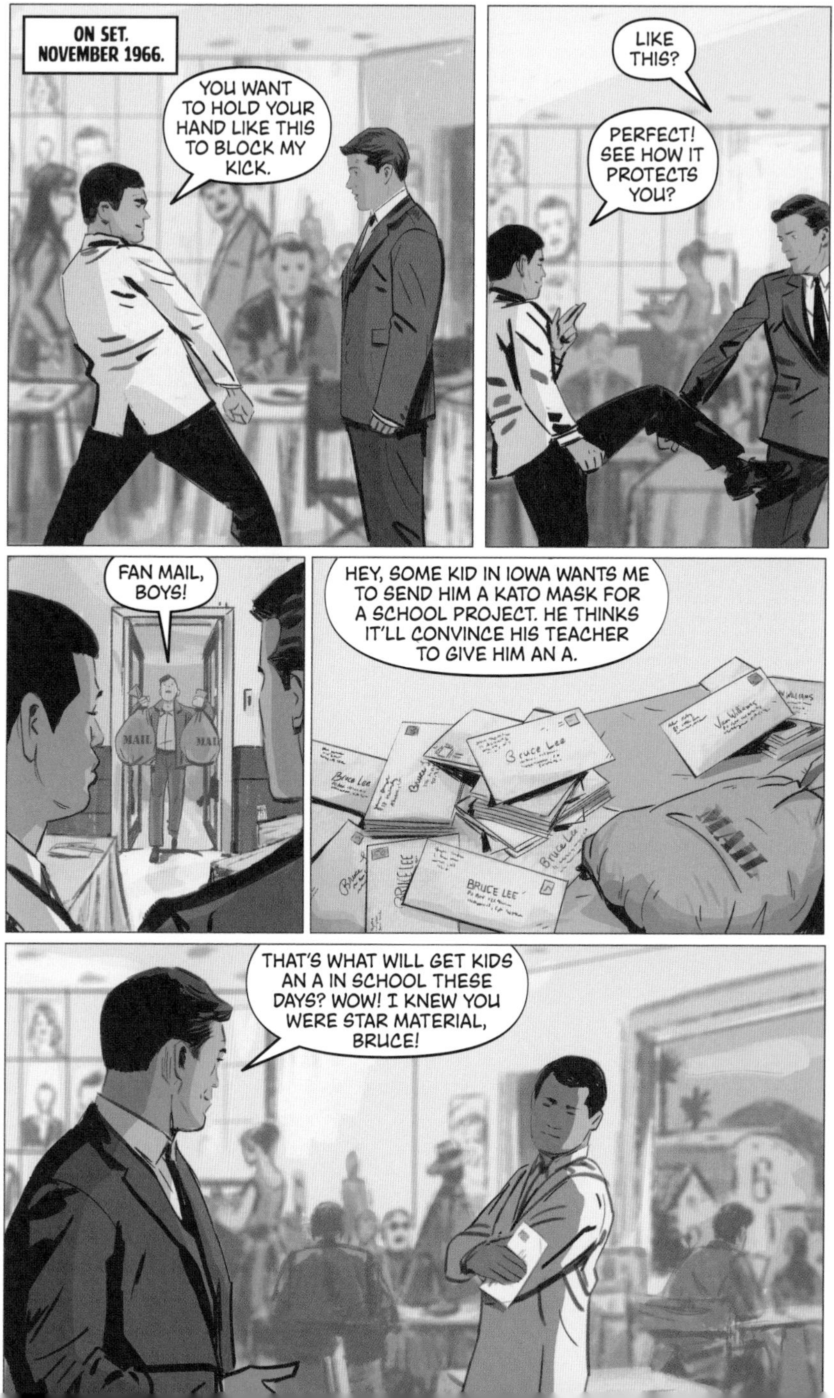
ON SET. NOVEMBER 1966.
YOU WANT TO HOLD YOUR HAND LIKE THIS TO BLOCK MY KICK.
LIKE THIS?
PERFECT! SEE HOW IT PROTECTS YOU?
FAN MAIL, BOYS!
HEY, SOME KID IN IOWA WANTS ME TO SEND HIM A KATO MASK FOR A SCHOOL PROJECT. HE THINKS IT'LL CONVINCE HIS TEACHER TO GIVE HIM AN A.
THAT'S WHAT WILL GET KIDS AN A IN SCHOOL THESE DAYS? WOW! I KNEW YOU WERE STAR MATERIAL, BRUCE!

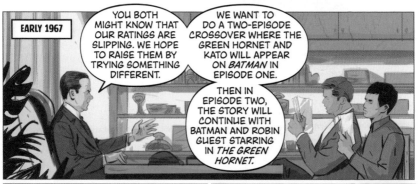

EARLY 1967

YOU BOTH MIGHT KNOW THAT OUR RATINGS ARE SLIPPING. WE HOPE TO RAISE THEM BY TRYING SOMETHING DIFFERENT.

WE WANT TO DO A TWO-EPISODE CROSSOVER WHERE THE GREEN HORNET AND KATO WILL APPEAR ON *BATMAN* IN EPISODE ONE.

THEN IN EPISODE TWO, THE STORY WILL CONTINUE WITH BATMAN AND ROBIN GUEST STARRING IN *THE GREEN HORNET*.

WHEN ARE THESE EPISODES GOING TO AIR?

EARLY MARCH, BEFORE THE NETWORK MAKES A DECISION ABOUT RENEWING THE SHOW.

IN THE STORY, THE GREEN HORNET AND KATO ARE VISITING GOTHAM CITY FOR A CONVENTION. THEY STUMBLE UPON A CRIME AND SWING INTO ACTION. BUT BATMAN AND ROBIN SHOW UP AND MISTAKE THEM FOR THE CRIMINALS.

A BIG FIGHT ENSUES, UNTIL EVERYONE REALIZES THEY'RE ON THE SAME SIDE, AND THEY FIGHT THE REAL CRIMINALS TOGETHER.

IT SAYS HERE THAT WE LOSE THE BRAWL TO BATMAN AND ROBIN!

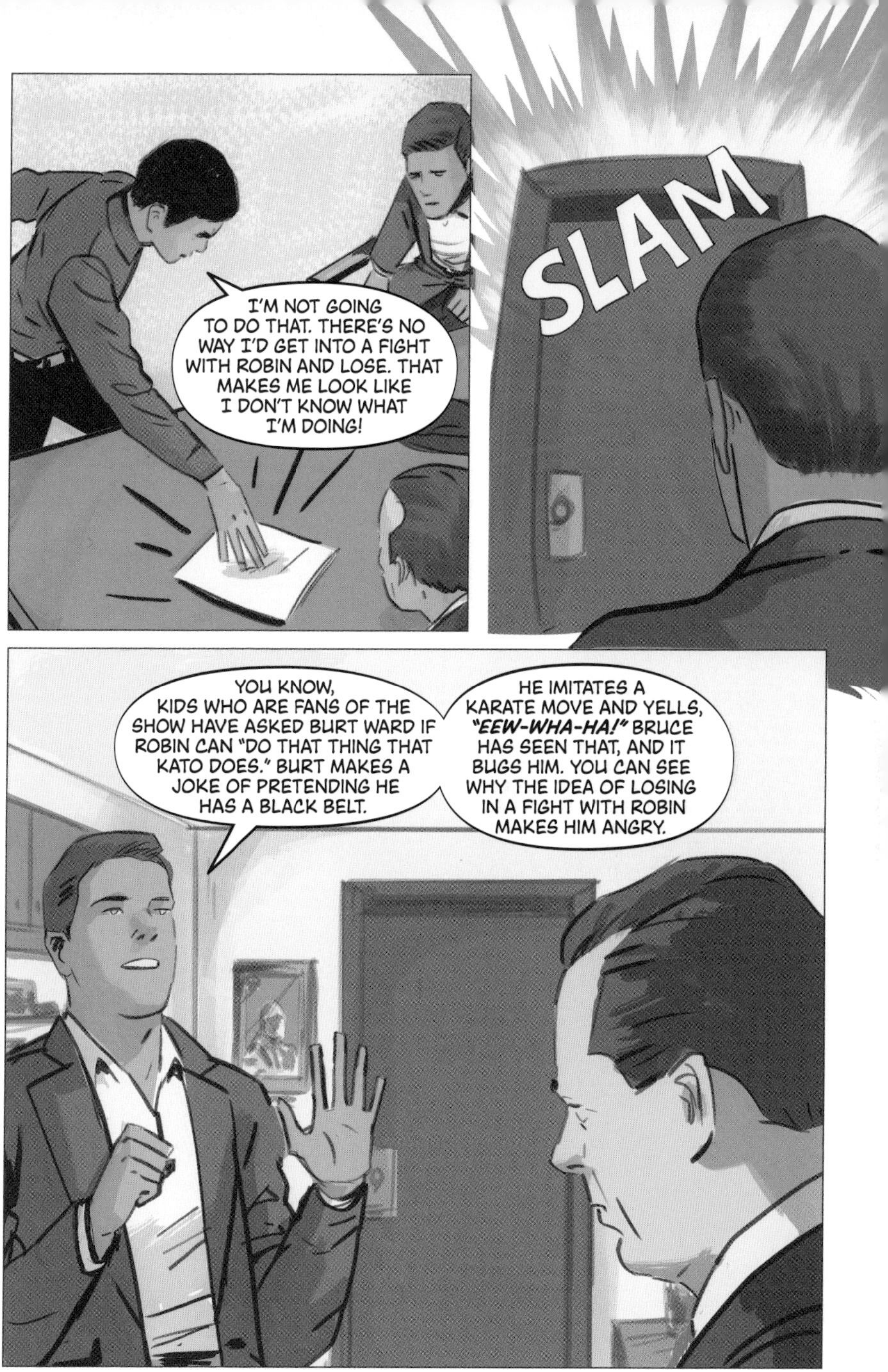
I'M NOT GOING TO DO THAT. THERE'S NO WAY I'D GET INTO A FIGHT WITH ROBIN AND LOSE. THAT MAKES ME LOOK LIKE I DON'T KNOW WHAT I'M DOING!
SLAM
YOU KNOW, KIDS WHO ARE FANS OF THE SHOW HAVE ASKED BURT WARD IF ROBIN CAN "DO THAT THING THAT KATO DOES." BURT MAKES A JOKE OF PRETENDING HE HAS A BLACK BELT.
HE IMITATES A KARATE MOVE AND YELLS, ***"EEW-WHA-HA!"*** BRUCE HAS SEEN THAT, AND IT BUGS HIM. YOU CAN SEE WHY THE IDEA OF LOSING IN A FIGHT WITH ROBIN MAKES HIM ANGRY.

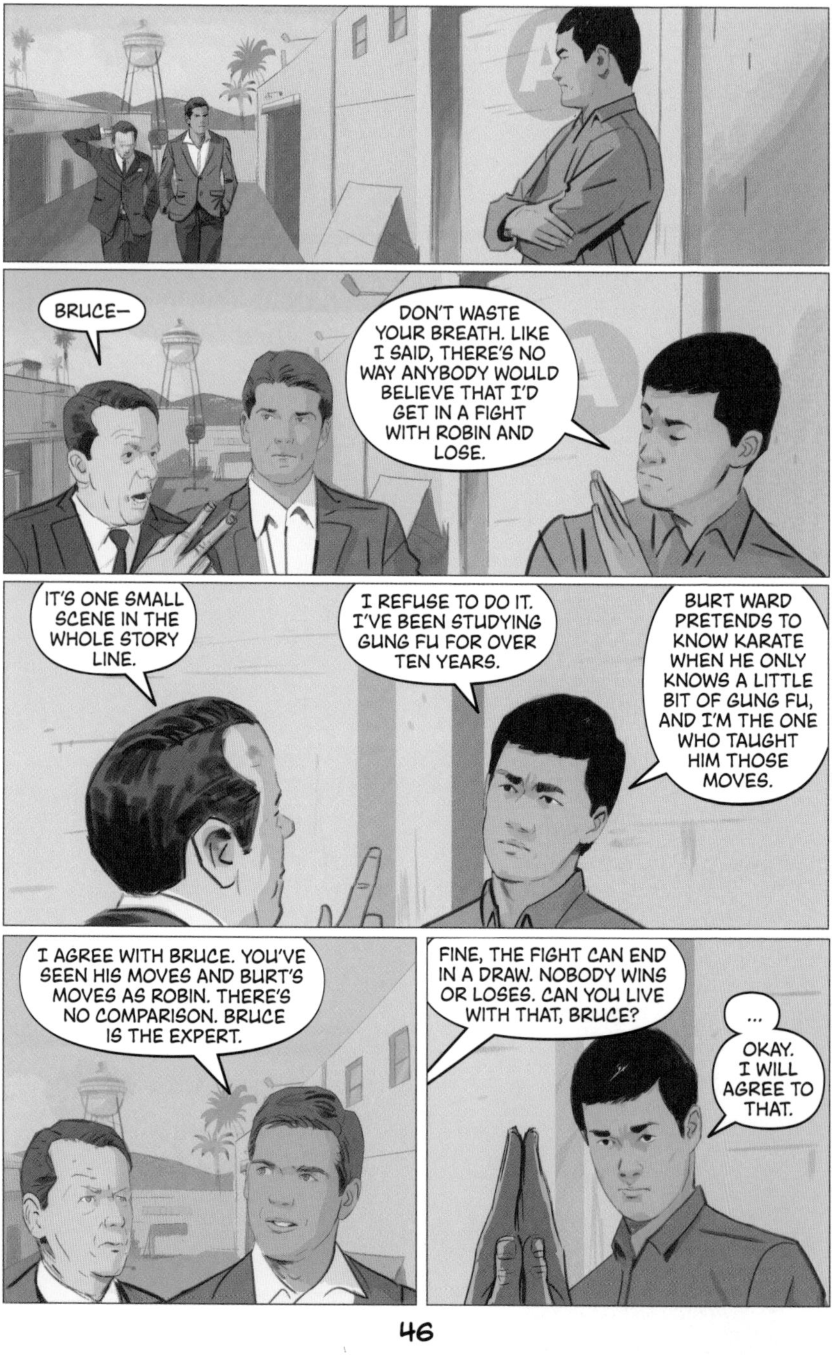
BRUCE—
DON'T WASTE YOUR BREATH. LIKE I SAID, THERE'S NO WAY ANYBODY WOULD BELIEVE THAT I'D GET IN A FIGHT WITH ROBIN AND LOSE.
IT'S ONE SMALL SCENE IN THE WHOLE STORY LINE.
I REFUSE TO DO IT. I'VE BEEN STUDYING GUNG FU FOR OVER TEN YEARS.
BURT WARD PRETENDS TO KNOW KARATE WHEN HE ONLY KNOWS A LITTLE BIT OF GUNG FU, AND I'M THE ONE WHO TAUGHT HIM THOSE MOVES.
I AGREE WITH BRUCE. YOU'VE SEEN HIS MOVES AND BURT'S MOVES AS ROBIN. THERE'S NO COMPARISON. BRUCE IS THE EXPERT.
FINE, THE FIGHT CAN END IN A DRAW. NOBODY WINS OR LOSES. CAN YOU LIVE WITH THAT, BRUCE?
...
OKAY. I WILL AGREE TO THAT.

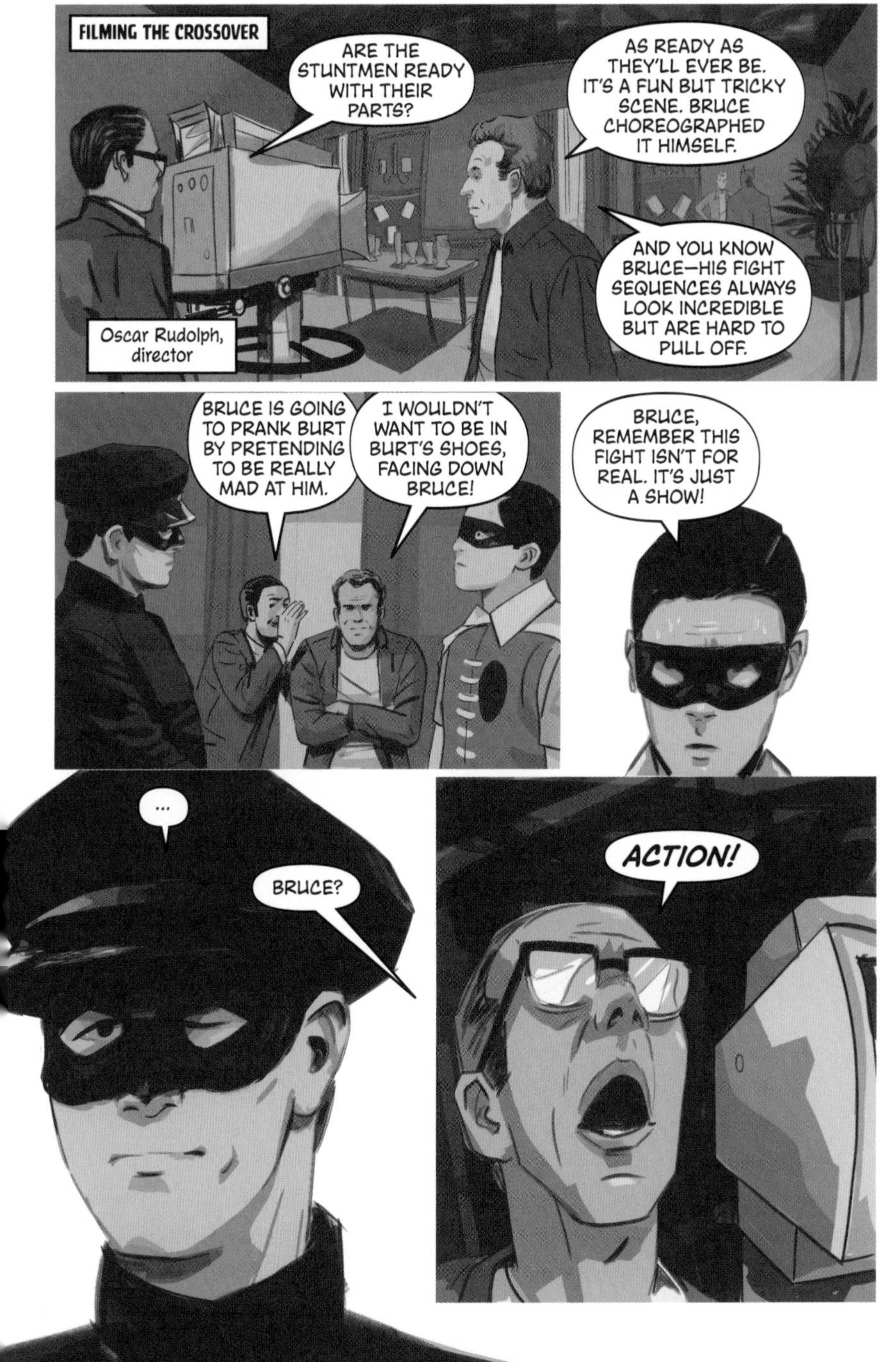
FILMING THE CROSSOVER
ARE THE STUNTMEN READY WITH THEIR PARTS?
AS READY AS THEY'LL EVER BE. IT'S A FUN BUT TRICKY SCENE. BRUCE CHOREOGRAPHED IT HIMSELF.
AND YOU KNOW BRUCE—HIS FIGHT SEQUENCES ALWAYS LOOK INCREDIBLE BUT ARE HARD TO PULL OFF.
Oscar Rudolph, director
BRUCE IS GOING TO PRANK BURT BY PRETENDING TO BE REALLY MAD AT HIM.
I WOULDN'T WANT TO BE IN BURT'S SHOES, FACING DOWN BRUCE!
BRUCE, REMEMBER THIS FIGHT ISN'T FOR REAL. IT'S JUST A SHOW!
...
BRUCE?
ACTION!

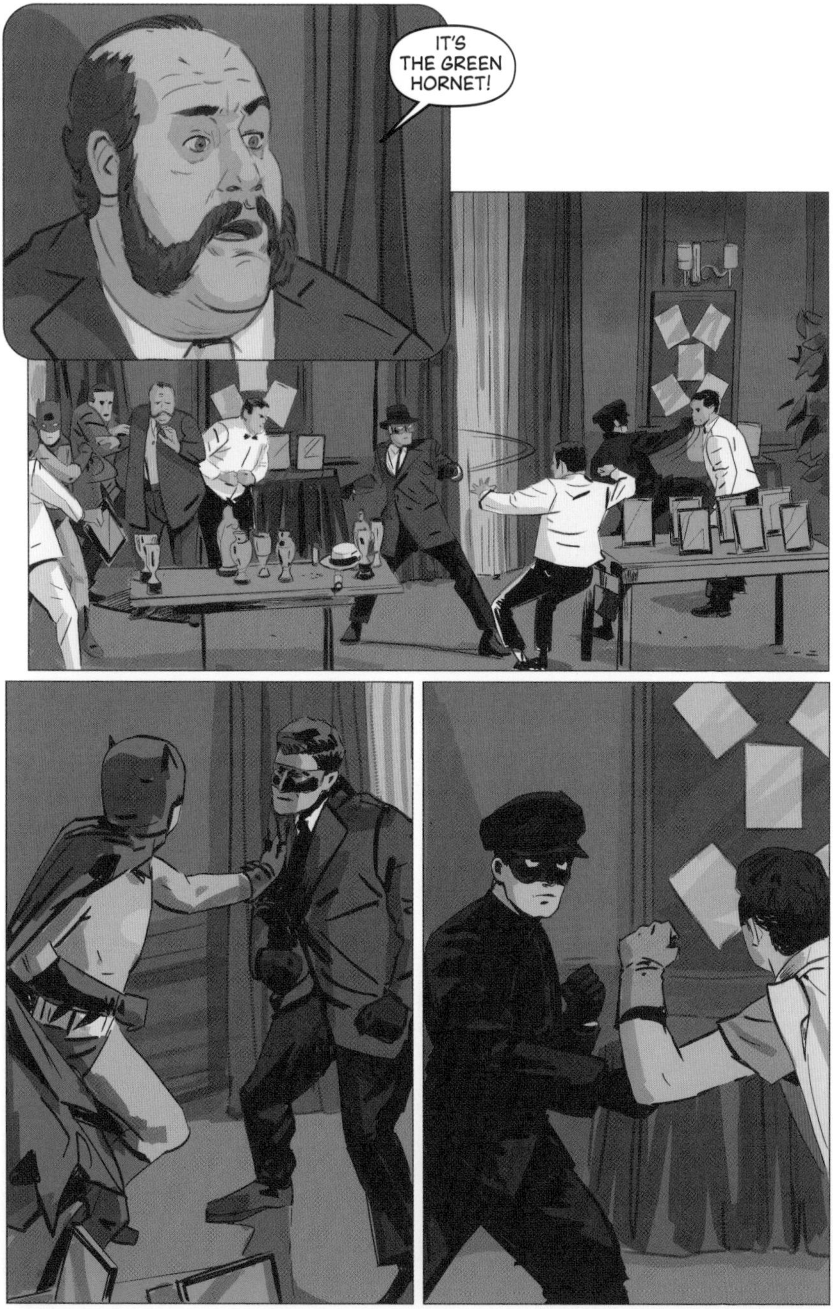
IT'S THE GREEN HORNET!

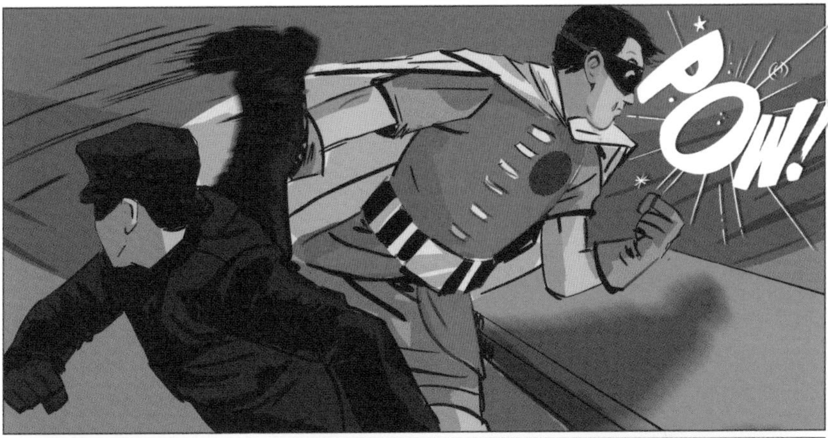
POW!

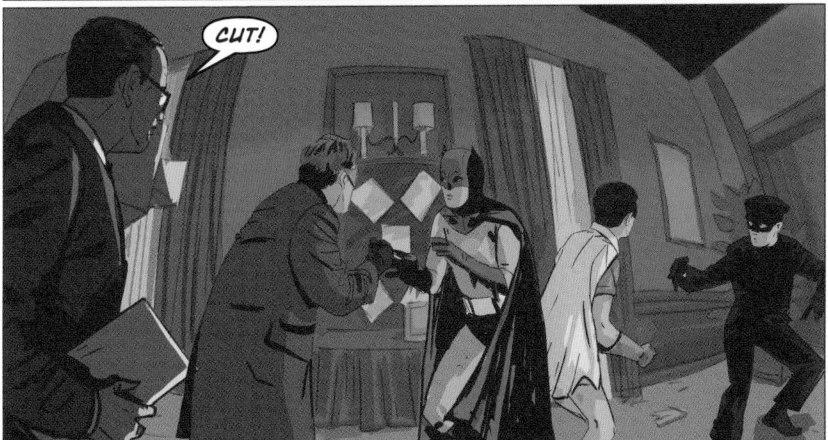
CUT!

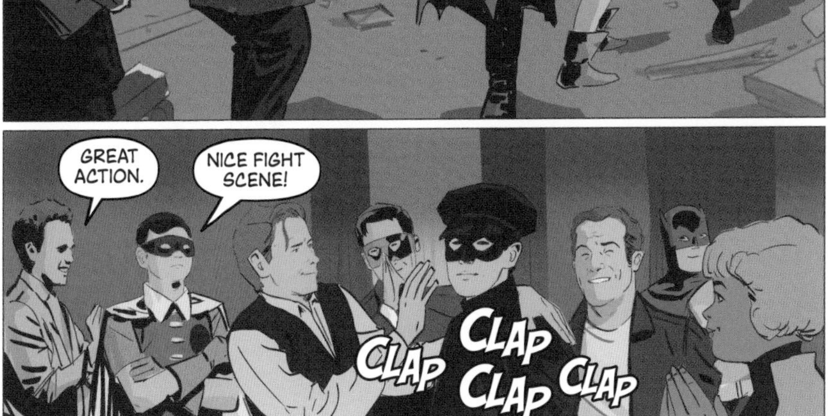
GREAT ACTION.
NICE FIGHT SCENE!
CLAP
CLAP
CLAP
CLAP

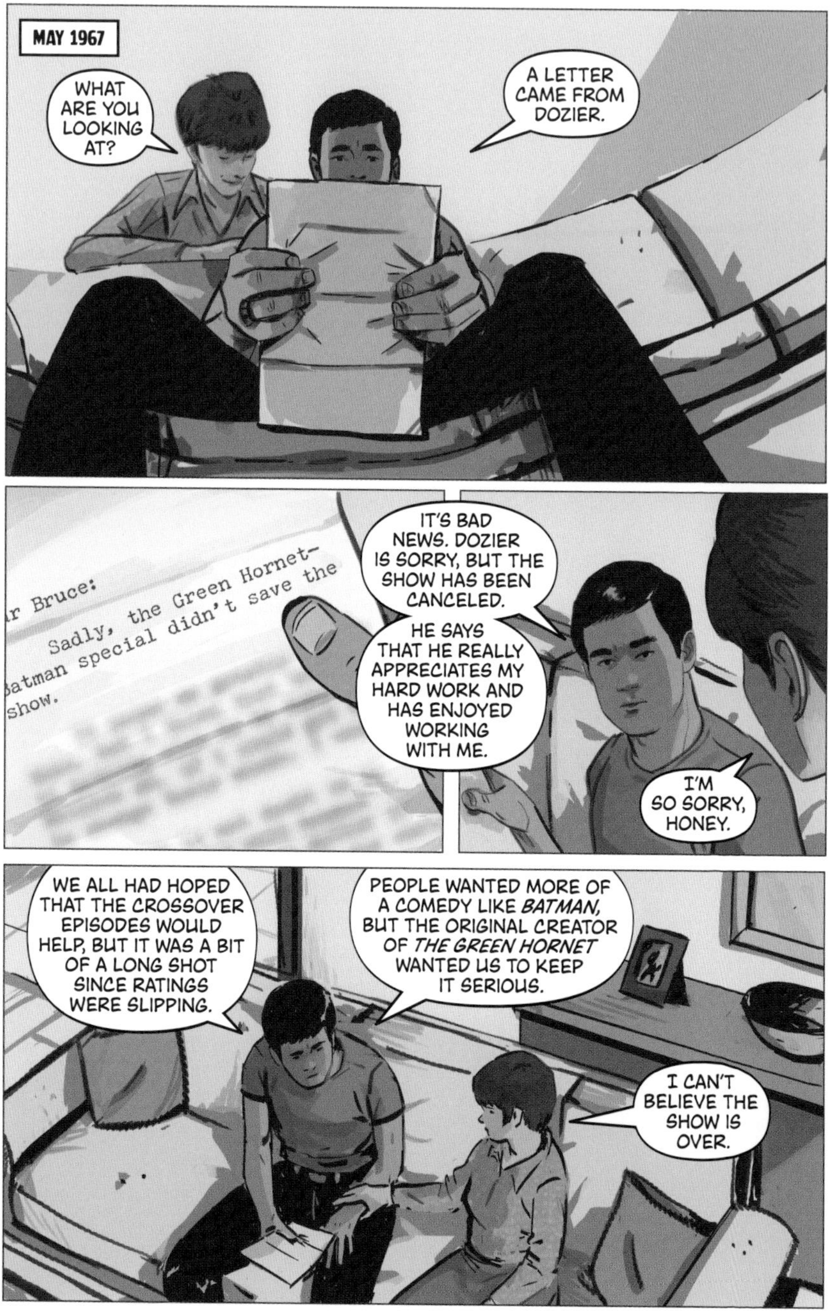
MAY 1967
WHAT ARE YOU LOOKING AT?
A LETTER CAME FROM DOZIER.
r Bruce:
Sadly, the Green Hornet-
Batman special didn't save the
show.
IT'S BAD NEWS. DOZIER IS SORRY, BUT THE SHOW HAS BEEN CANCELED.
HE SAYS THAT HE REALLY APPRECIATES MY HARD WORK AND HAS ENJOYED WORKING WITH ME.
I'M SO SORRY, HONEY.
WE ALL HAD HOPED THAT THE CROSSOVER EPISODES WOULD HELP, BUT IT WAS A BIT OF A LONG SHOT SINCE RATINGS WERE SLIPPING.
PEOPLE WANTED MORE OF A COMEDY LIKE *BATMAN*, BUT THE ORIGINAL CREATOR OF *THE GREEN HORNET* WANTED US TO KEEP IT SERIOUS.
I CAN'T BELIEVE THE SHOW IS OVER.

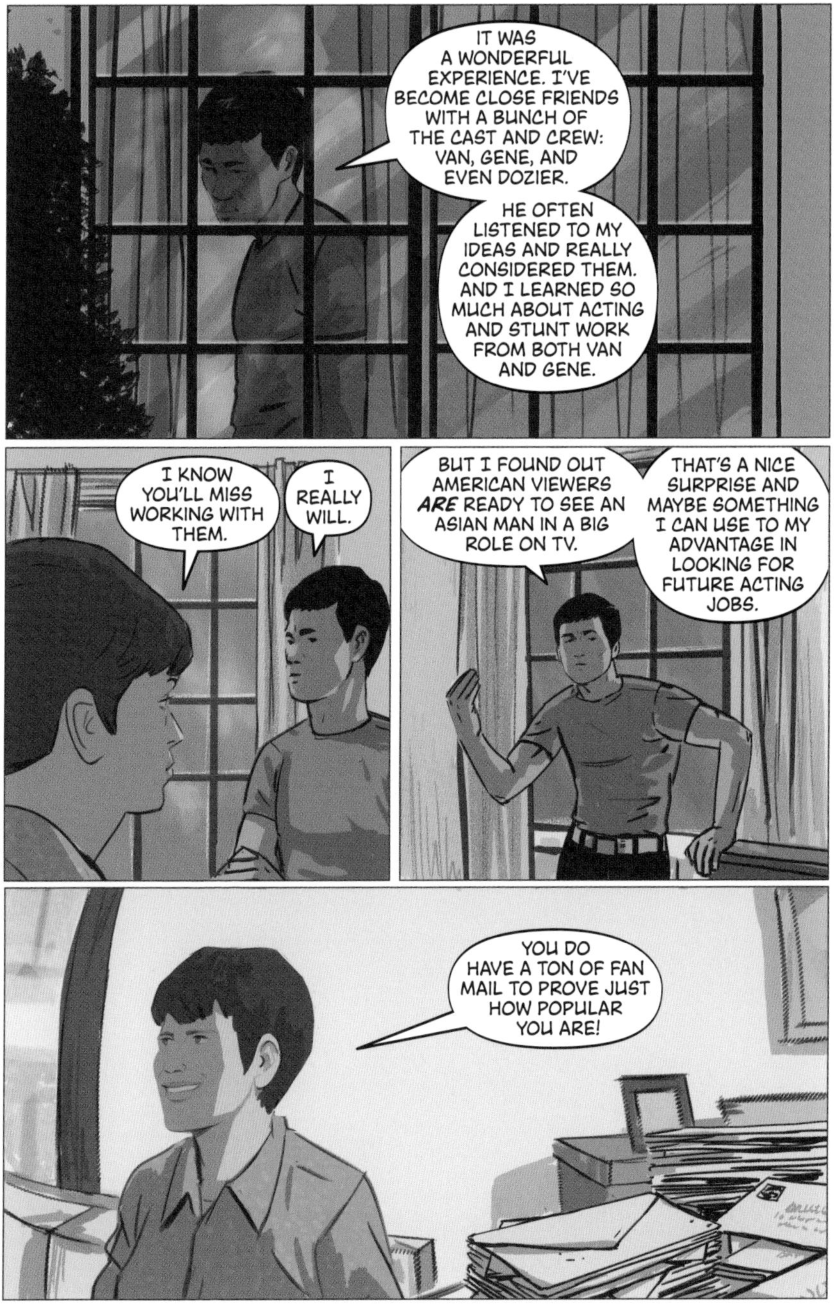
IT WAS A WONDERFUL EXPERIENCE. I'VE BECOME CLOSE FRIENDS WITH A BUNCH OF THE CAST AND CREW: VAN, GENE, AND EVEN DOZIER.
HE OFTEN LISTENED TO MY IDEAS AND REALLY CONSIDERED THEM. AND I LEARNED SO MUCH ABOUT ACTING AND STUNT WORK FROM BOTH VAN AND GENE.
I KNOW YOU'LL MISS WORKING WITH THEM.
I REALLY WILL.
BUT I FOUND OUT AMERICAN VIEWERS *ARE* READY TO SEE AN ASIAN MAN IN A BIG ROLE ON TV.
THAT'S A NICE SURPRISE AND MAYBE SOMETHING I CAN USE TO MY ADVANTAGE IN LOOKING FOR FUTURE ACTING JOBS.
YOU DO HAVE A TON OF FAN MAIL TO PROVE JUST HOW POPULAR YOU ARE!

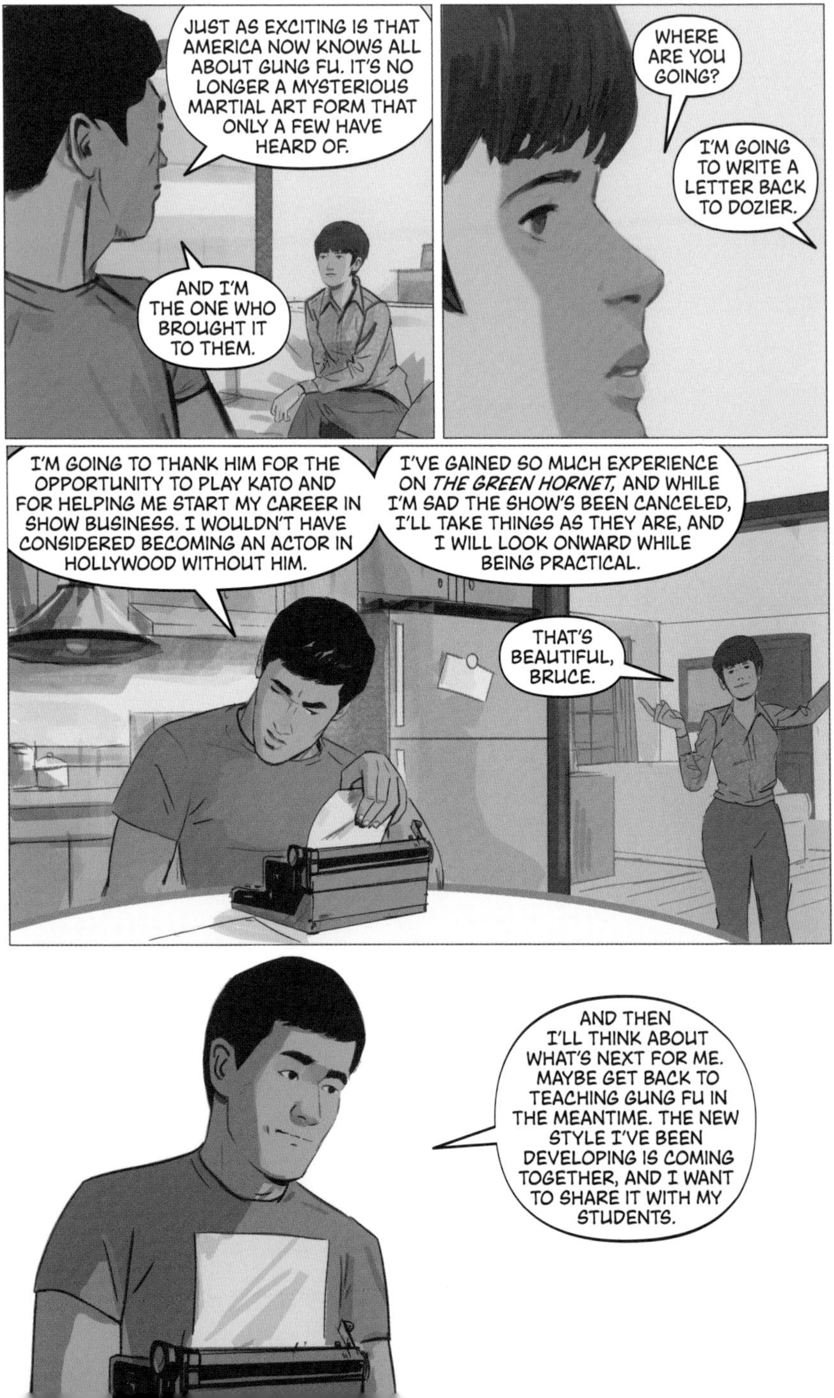
JUST AS EXCITING IS THAT AMERICA NOW KNOWS ALL ABOUT GUNG FU. IT'S NO LONGER A MYSTERIOUS MARTIAL ART FORM THAT ONLY A FEW HAVE HEARD OF.
AND I'M THE ONE WHO BROUGHT IT TO THEM.
WHERE ARE YOU GOING?
I'M GOING TO WRITE A LETTER BACK TO DOZIER.
I'M GOING TO THANK HIM FOR THE OPPORTUNITY TO PLAY KATO AND FOR HELPING ME START MY CAREER IN SHOW BUSINESS. I WOULDN'T HAVE CONSIDERED BECOMING AN ACTOR IN HOLLYWOOD WITHOUT HIM.
I'VE GAINED SO MUCH EXPERIENCE ON *THE GREEN HORNET,* AND WHILE I'M SAD THE SHOW'S BEEN CANCELED, I'LL TAKE THINGS AS THEY ARE, AND I WILL LOOK ONWARD WHILE BEING PRACTICAL.
THAT'S BEAUTIFUL, BRUCE.
AND THEN I'LL THINK ABOUT WHAT'S NEXT FOR ME. MAYBE GET BACK TO TEACHING GUNG FU IN THE MEANTIME. THE NEW STYLE I'VE BEEN DEVELOPING IS COMING TOGETHER, AND I WANT TO SHARE IT WITH MY STUDENTS.

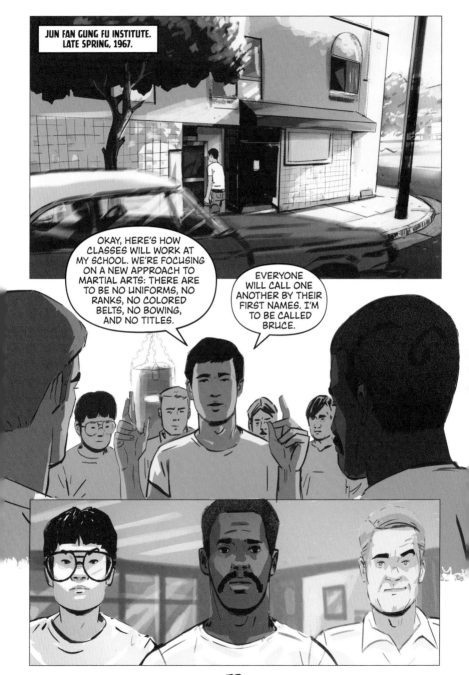

JUN FAN GUNG FU INSTITUTE. LATE SPRING, 1967.

OKAY, HERE'S HOW CLASSES WILL WORK AT MY SCHOOL. WE'RE FOCUSING ON A NEW APPROACH TO MARTIAL ARTS: THERE ARE TO BE NO UNIFORMS, NO RANKS, NO COLORED BELTS, NO BOWING, AND NO TITLES.

EVERYONE WILL CALL ONE ANOTHER BY THEIR FIRST NAMES. I'M TO BE CALLED BRUCE.

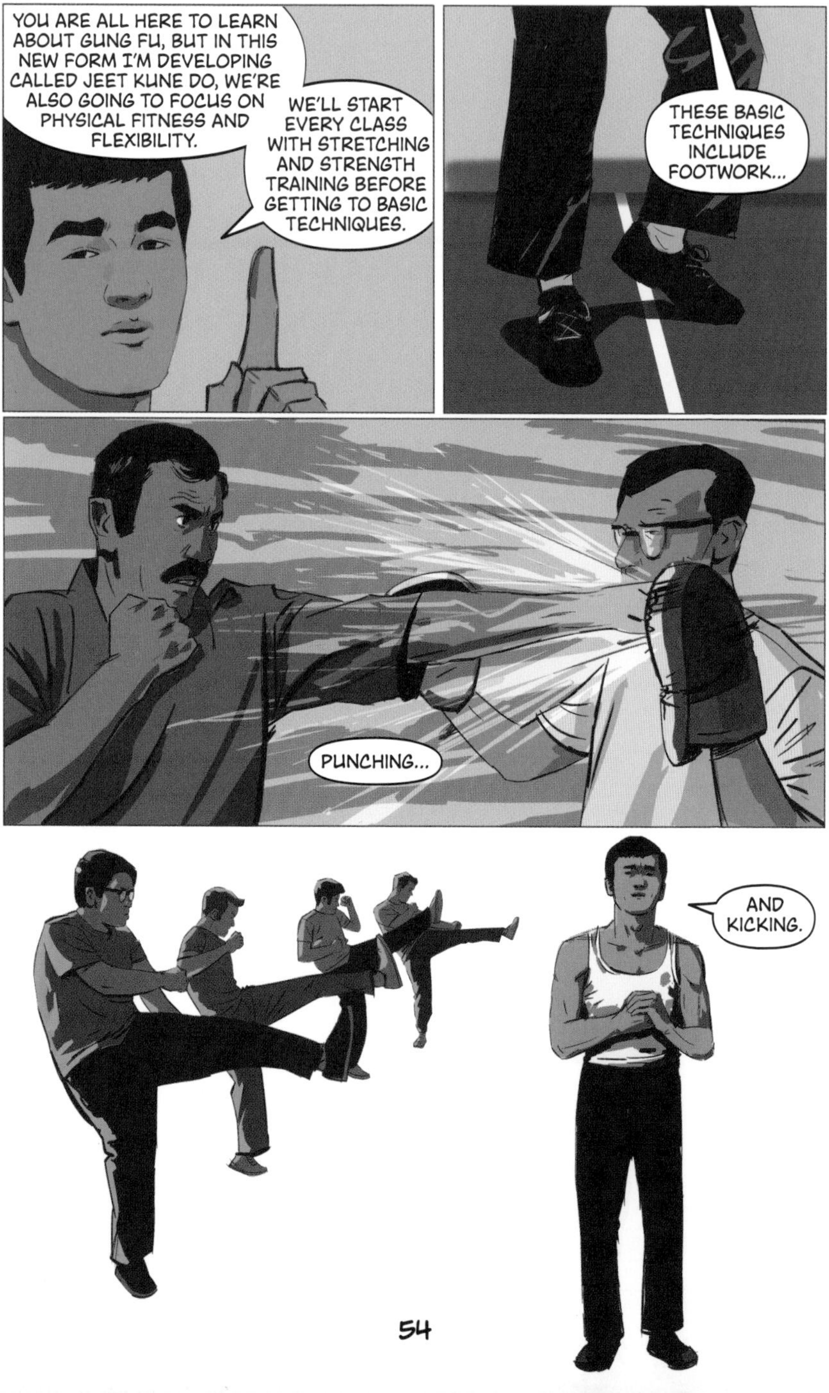
YOU ARE ALL HERE TO LEARN ABOUT GUNG FU, BUT IN THIS NEW FORM I'M DEVELOPING CALLED JEET KUNE DO, WE'RE ALSO GOING TO FOCUS ON PHYSICAL FITNESS AND FLEXIBILITY.
WE'LL START EVERY CLASS WITH STRETCHING AND STRENGTH TRAINING BEFORE GETTING TO BASIC TECHNIQUES.
THESE BASIC TECHNIQUES INCLUDE FOOTWORK...
PUNCHING...
AND KICKING.

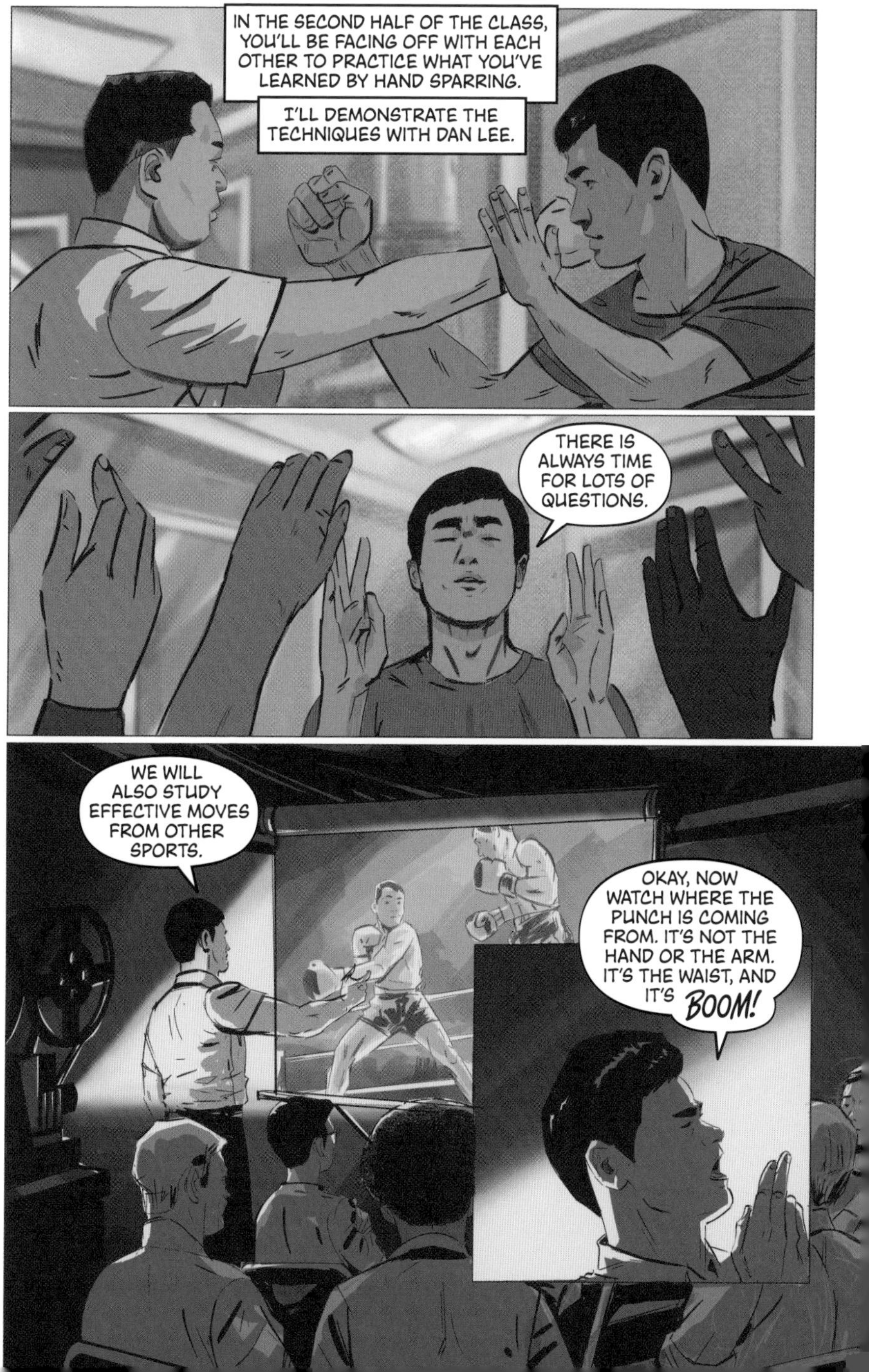
IN THE SECOND HALF OF THE CLASS, YOU'LL BE FACING OFF WITH EACH OTHER TO PRACTICE WHAT YOU'VE LEARNED BY HAND SPARRING.
I'LL DEMONSTRATE THE TECHNIQUES WITH DAN LEE.
THERE IS ALWAYS TIME FOR LOTS OF QUESTIONS.
WE WILL ALSO STUDY EFFECTIVE MOVES FROM OTHER SPORTS.
OKAY, NOW WATCH WHERE THE PUNCH IS COMING FROM. IT'S NOT THE HAND OR THE ARM. IT'S THE WAIST, AND IT'S BOOM!

Jeet Kune Do

Translated as the "Way of the Intercepting Fist," Jeet Kune Do was invented by Bruce Lee over a number of years as he discovered that the Wing Chun form of gung fu wasn't suitable in all types of fights.

截拳道 literally means "stop fist way." The idea came from a fencing technique called "stop hit." Bruce described Jeet Kune Do in his notes as "fencing without a sword."

Combining elements from fencing, boxing, gung fu, and other martial arts, Bruce created Jeet Kune Do as a way to stop an opponent—to "intercept his movement, his thoughts, or his motive"—before the attack.

Many people practice Jeet Kune Do today, but there may never be anyone as good at it as Bruce. As one of his first students once noted, Bruce could sense a potential movement before it happened, but can the average person do the same?

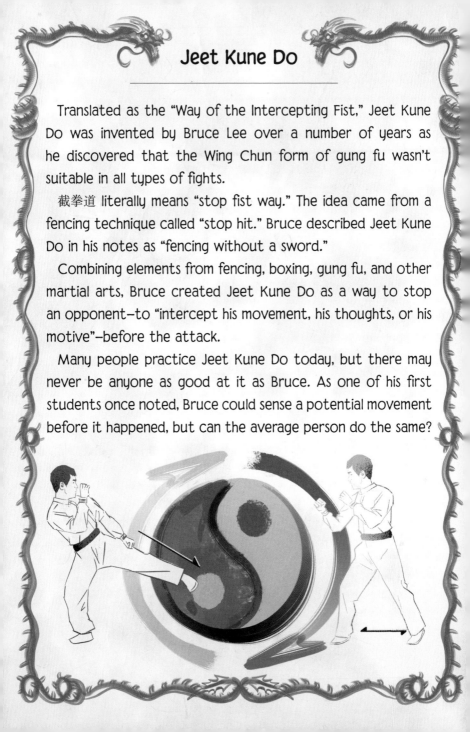

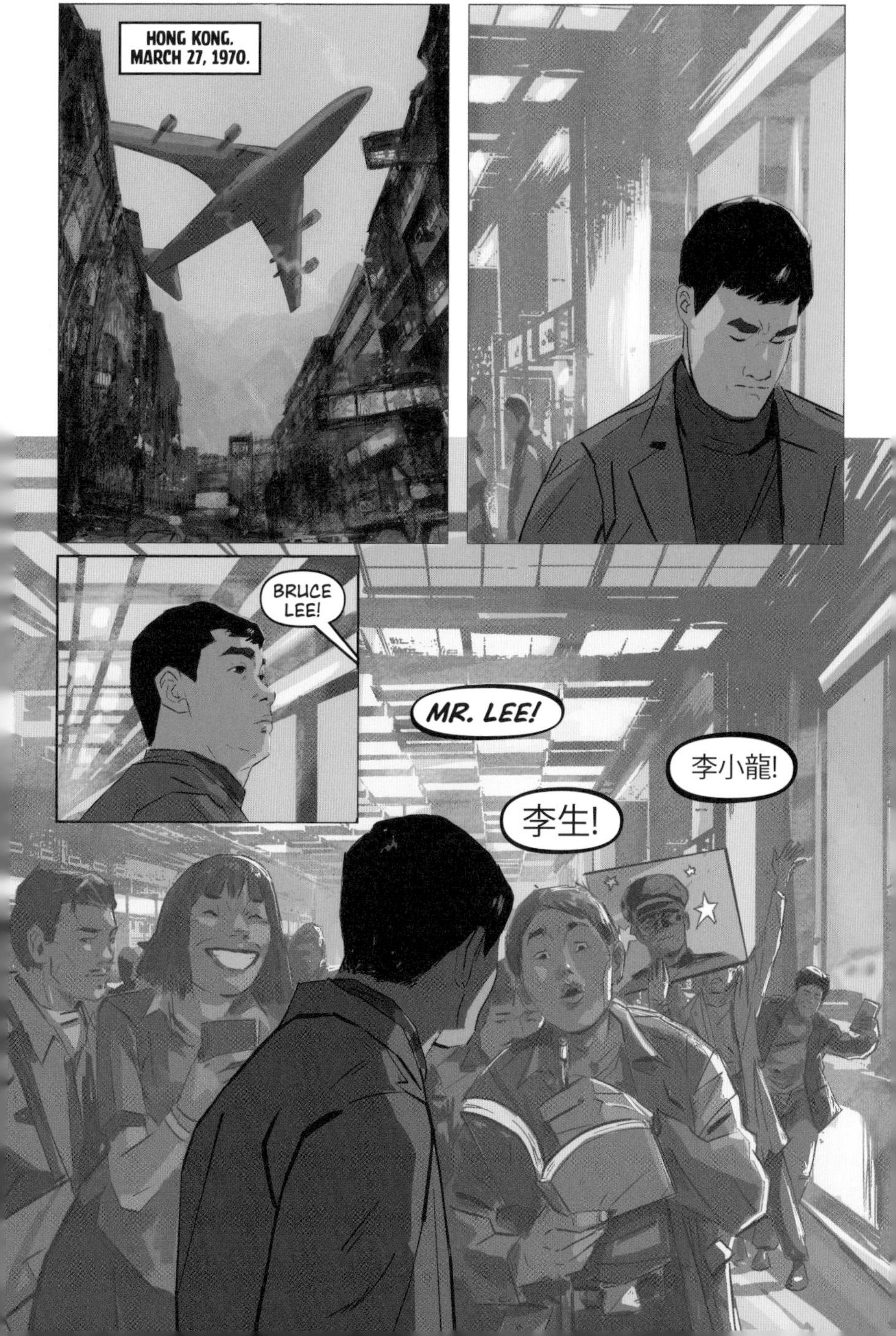
HONG KONG.
MARCH 27, 1970.
BRUCE LEE!
MR. LEE!
李小龍!
李生!

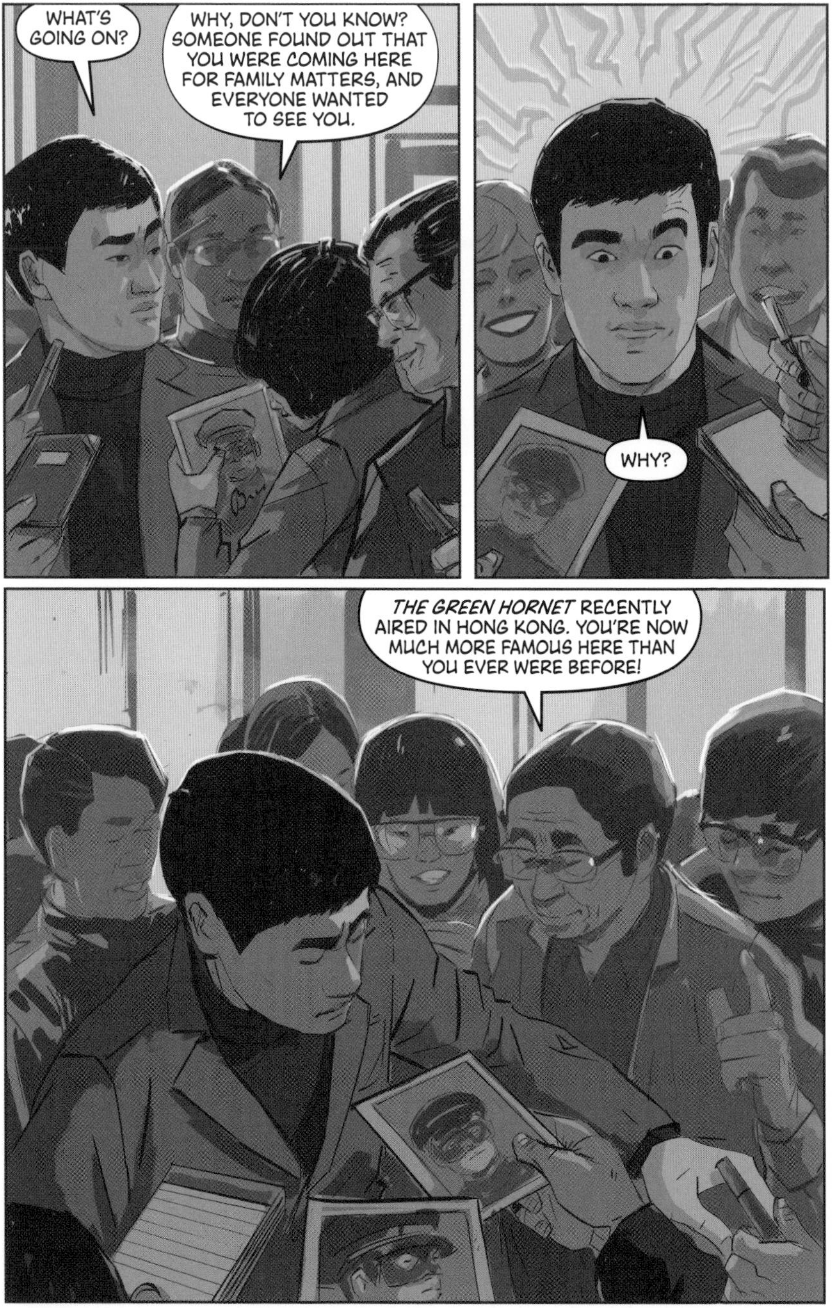
WHAT'S GOING ON?
WHY, DON'T YOU KNOW? SOMEONE FOUND OUT THAT YOU WERE COMING HERE FOR FAMILY MATTERS, AND EVERYONE WANTED TO SEE YOU.
WHY?
THE GREEN HORNET RECENTLY AIRED IN HONG KONG. YOU'RE NOW MUCH MORE FAMOUS HERE THAN YOU EVER WERE BEFORE!

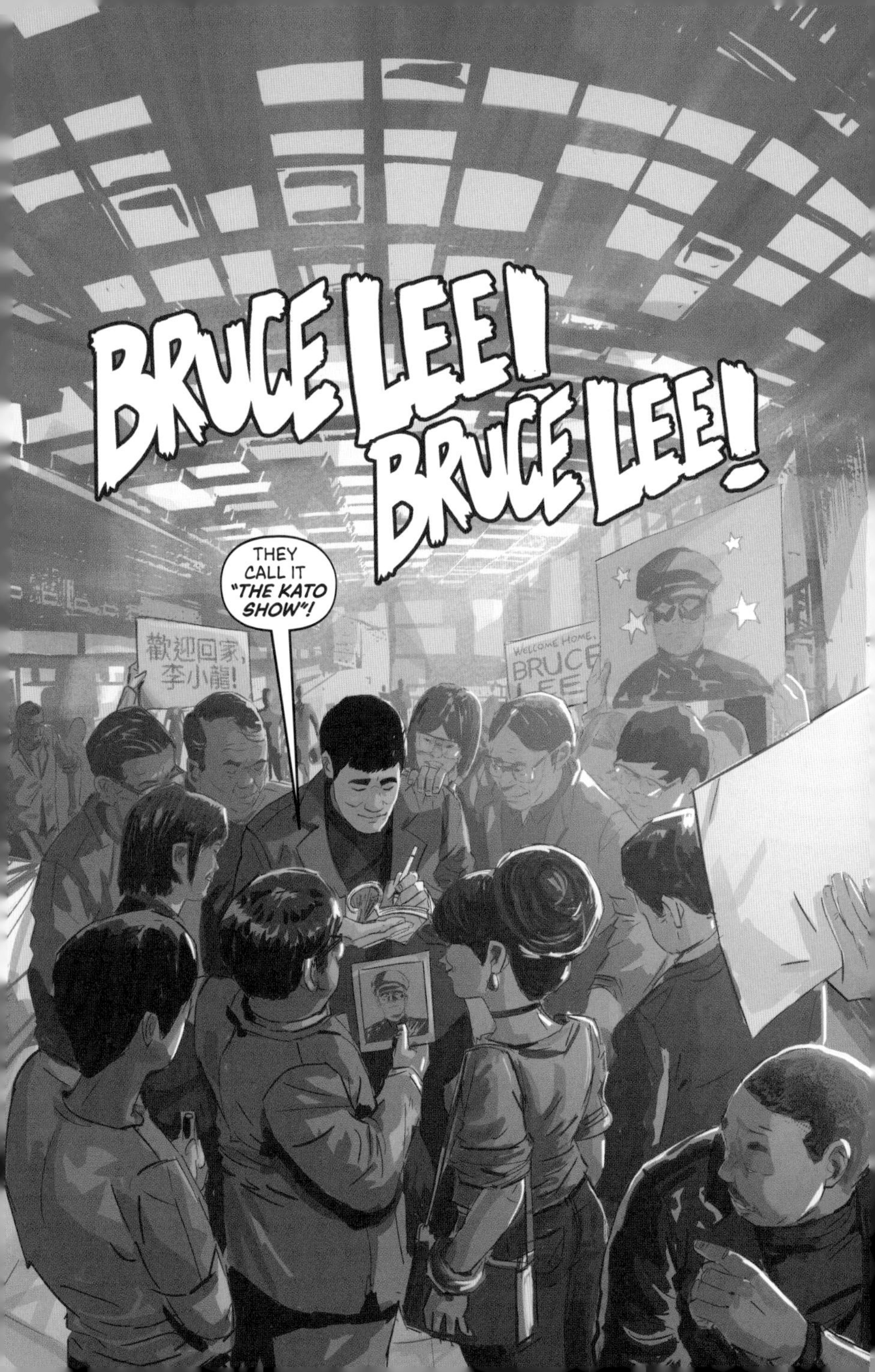
BRUCE LEE! BRUCE LEE!
THEY CALL IT "THE KATO SHOW"!
歡迎回家,
李小龍!
WELCOME HOME,
BRUCE
LEE

Conclusion

In his celebrated 1970 return to his childhood hometown, Bruce Lee was welcomed as a star. His fame and reputation as a Chinese person who'd made it in Hollywood became a source of pride for Chinese people everywhere. He represented a blend of East and West that appealed to people all over the world.

Now that Bruce had Hollywood experience, Hong Kong movie executives were eager to sign him for projects. Bruce wanted to work with them, too, since he was tired of waiting on nonexistent lead roles for him back in America. With these Hong Kong studios, he starred in several martial arts movies: *The Big Boss*, *Fist of Fury*, *The Way of the Dragon*, *Enter the Dragon*, and *Game of Death*.

The films turned out to be hugely popular worldwide, breaking box-office records and making Bruce Lee a household name.

Tragically, Bruce died while he was filming *Game of Death* due to causes that still are not entirely known.

In his short life, Bruce Lee had a huge impact globally, but especially in America—becoming the first Asian man to play the main supporting role on a TV show, being the first true martial arts expert in Hollywood, and making gung fu famous across the nation. His accomplishments were made possible due to his boundless energy, determination, hard work, and dedication to his principles. In his book, *Tao of Jeet Kune Do*, he wrote:

"Jeet Kune Do is the enlightenment. It is a way of life, a movement toward willpower and control, though it ought to be enlightened by intuition."

Willpower, self-control, and intuition—these qualities made Bruce Lee the person that many people admire today, even decades after his death.

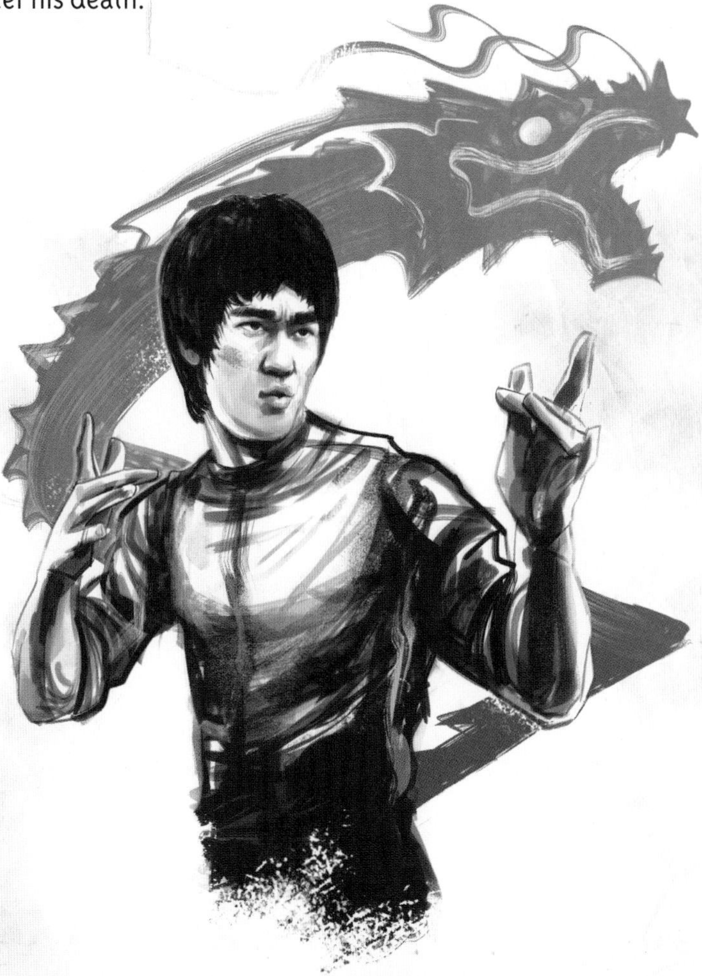

Timeline of Bruce Lee's Life

1940 — Bruce Lee is born on November 27 in San Francisco, California, during the Year of the Dragon according to the Chinese zodiac

1941 — Bruce and his parents return to Hong Kong

1953 — Begins Wing Chun gung fu lessons

1959 — Moves back to the United States

1964 — Marries Linda Emery

— Performs at the International Karate Championships at Long Beach, California

1965 — Birth of son, Brandon Lee

1966 — Portrays Kato in *The Green Hornet* television series

1967 — *The Green Hornet* series ends

— Bruce opens Jun Fan Gung Fu Institute in Los Angeles, California

— Names his new martial art approach Jeet Kune Do

1969 — Birth of daughter, Shannon Lee

1970 — Visits Hong Kong in March and is greeted by an adoring crowd

1971 — Stars in *The Big Boss*

1972 — Stars in *Fist of Fury* and *The Way of the Dragon*

1973 — Stars in *Enter the Dragon*

— Dies on July 20 while filming *Game of Death*

Bibliography

*Books for young readers

*Amara, Philip, and Oliver Chin. ***Awesome Asian Americans: 20 Stars Who Made America Amazing***. CA: Immedium, 2020.

Clouse, Robert. ***Bruce Lee: The Biography***. Burbank, CA: Unique Publications, 1988.

*Di Bartolo, Jim. ***The Boy Who Became a Dragon: A Bruce Lee Story***. New York: Graphix/Scholastic, 2020.

*Gigliotti, Jim. ***Who Was Bruce Lee?*** New York: Penguin Workshop, 2014.

Lee, Bruce. ***Tao of Jeet Kune Do***. Valencia, CA: Black Belt Books, 2011.

*Pawlak, Debra Ann. ***Bruce Lee***. Philadelphia, PA: Mason Crest Publishers, 2008.

Polly, Matthew. ***Bruce Lee: A Life***. New York: Simon & Schuster, 2018.

Qi, Li Wen, dir. ***Legend of Bruce Lee. Volume 1, 2, 3***. Plano, TX: Well Go USA Entertainment, 2016, 2017. DVD.

ABOUT THE CREATORS

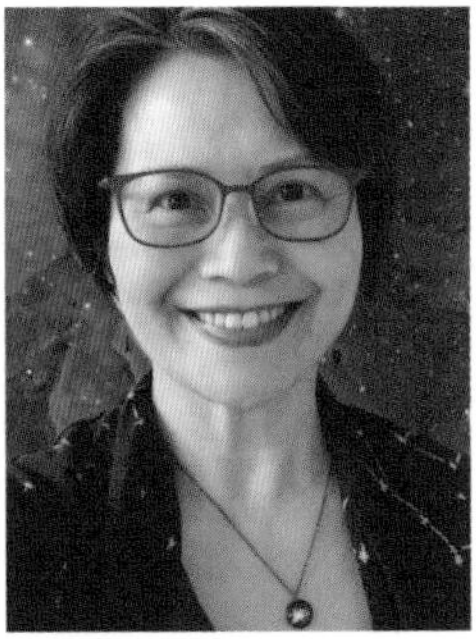

Teresa Robeson is the APALA Picture Book Award–winning author of *Queen of Physics*, *Two Bicycles in Beijing*, *Who Is Tibet's Exiled Leader? The 14th Dalai Lama*, and *Clouds in Space: Nebulae, Stardust, and Us*. Her upcoming works include a picture book about a beloved Chinese holiday and two fun nonfiction middle-grade books. Teresa was born in Hong Kong and, like Bruce Lee, grew up there. Unlike Bruce Lee, she is not very good at gung fu, but she could fend off a mean rooster on her family's mini farm if she had to. Visit her online at teresarobeson.com.

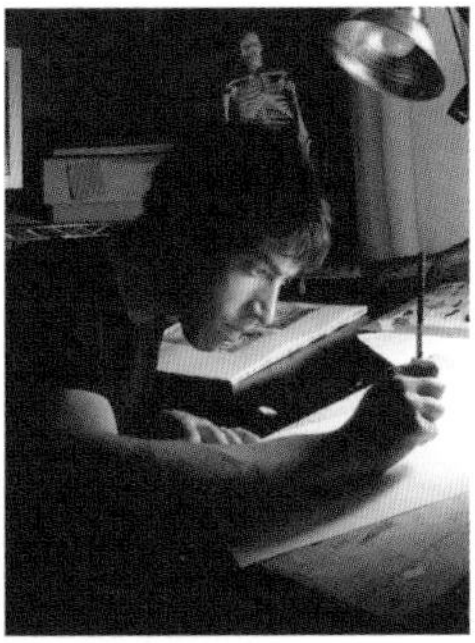

YUKO INZANA

Ryan Inzana is an illustrator/concept designer/animator whose work has appeared in various media all over the world. Ryan's comics have been inducted into the Library of Congress's permanent collection of art, and his graphic novel *Ichiro* earned an Eisner nomination as well as an Asian American/Pacific Islander Honor Award for YA literature. You can visit Ryan online at ryaninzana.com or follow him on Instagram @ryan_inzana.